H. CECIL PAWSON

Personal Evangelism

1908 Grand Avenue

Nashville, Tennessee 37203

© H. CECIL PAWSON 1968
FIRST PUBLISHED IN 1968
BY EPWORTH PRESS
Book Steward: Frank Cumbers

SBN 7162 0040 6

Personal Evangelism

To
MY WIFE

AUTHOR'S PREFACE

I AM grateful to my friend, the Editor of the Epworth Press, for his invitation, entirely unexpected, to write this book, and for all his encouragement and help. I felt it to be a call of God, whilst also feeling utterly unworthy and inadequate for the task.

My greatest friend, now in heaven, the Rev. Dr W. E. Sangster, humbled me, yet encouraged me greatly, by dedicating his book on evangelism, *Let me Commend*, thus: 'To Cecil Pawson, an evangelist and the son of an evangelist.' I was never taught, but caught the glory of personal evangelism from my father; whilst my mother revealed in everything the Christ they both loved and served so faithfully to the end.

I have endeavoured many times to find adequate words with which to extend the dedication of this book, but have failed – the debt I owe to my wife is not only incalculable but beyond words. Throughout a blissfully happy married partnership of over forty years, she has done everything possible – often at much inconvenience and personal sacrifice – to co-operate in and complement my humble efforts in evangelistic service. Not only because of her patient translation of my almost illegible writing into typescript for this work, along with her helpful, constructive suggestions and amendments am I grateful, but still more for her constant encouragement and invaluable support in seeking to bring others into the Kingdom. In His glorious fellowship and service we share the peace that passeth understanding and the joy unspeakable.

I must mention, too, my sister, my two brothers (both now in heaven), and my children, whose prayers and keen interest in my evangelism have been used of God so wonderfully down the years.

Also to the loyal and devoted friends of my Men's Fellowship Group, which meets every Tuesday in the year, and has done so for thirty-six years and which I am privileged to lead, I am eternally grateful. I can only add that I have received far more from them in knowledge and experience of God and man, and of prayer and service in reaching non-Christians, than anything I have been able to give.

Three important convictions, therefore, confirmed in my work as a personal evangelist over a life-time, are firstly, that evangelism should be centred in the local church; secondly, that personal evangelism is most effective when it operates through a fellowship of prayer partners and 'co-workers together with God'; thirdly, that we can never hope to convert Britain until Christian laymen use the daily opportunities available to them for personal evangelism more fully.

It is my earnest prayer that this little book may be used of God to help to meet the need of every church today – namely an increase of personal evangelists of both clergy and laity working from within the church in a true priesthood of all believers.

1967   H. CECIL PAWSON

CONTENTS

Cardinal Heenan to Malcolm Muggeridge: 'Evangelists, men who have the message, which they believe to be true, and want to spread it everywhere. . . . If you're a good man and you possess a good thing you want to share it.'

(From *Muggeridge Through the Microphone* (1968), p. 122

CHAPTER ONE

MISSION

'Go ye into all the world and make Christians of all nations'
(Matthew 28.19, A.V. Marginal)

EVANGELISM is the expression of God's mission to the
world. God's mission of redeeming love is to bring His
children to know and love Him that they may do His
will on earth as it is done in heaven, and enjoy His
fellowship for ever. The fulfilment of this mission is to
be accomplished by obedience to Christ's commission
to all His followers, quoted from Matthew's Gospel at
the head of this chapter. This was the *final* commandment of Jesus to His disciples. If to become a Christian
means, as I believe, to respond to the love of Christ –
'lovest thou me' is the vital question He put to Peter,
which He asks of you and me – then the proof of such
responsive love lies in His words: 'If you love me, keep
my commandments.'

'Go ye into all the world . . .' as said to His earliest
followers, was translated into action mainly in a geographical sense, as witness Mark's concluding verse in his
Gospel: 'And they went forth and preached everywhere', and in a more exact description, by maps
showing the missionary journeys of St Paul. It was as
some of these earliest followers of Christ were obeying
His commission at Antioch that they received the
name (or nickname) which remains to this day: 'And

the disciples were called Christians first at Antioch.'

It is still the personal responsibility of the Christian to preach Christ everywhere, meaning the place and sphere of service which our varying activities embrace. Today, however, we should give a wider connotation to this word 'world'. There are worlds within the world and the mission of God concerns them all – hence the relevance of Christ's commission to all life's activities.

We sing of those worlds in John Ellerton's hymn:

> *Thine is the loom, the forge, the mart,*
> *The wealth of land and sea,*
> *The world of science and of art*
> *Revealed and ruled by Thee.*

In all these worlds the aim of the Christian is to seek first the Kingdom of God, the rule of God, and that is what he means when he prays: 'Thy Kingdom come. Thy will be done on earth.'

How greatly the Gospel – the good news of God and His loving purposes for all His children – is needed in *the world of education*. We have our wonderful new schools and equipment, and our expenditure on such continues to rise, and rightly so – the same applies to our universities and technical colleges and extra mural education. Rarely do we give the consideration merited by the simple question: 'What is the school for?' In earlier times a student came up to the University 'to study the glory of God', nowadays it is to work for the qualifications needed for the best possible means of earning a livelihood. Training for life which leaves God out of account can never attain the highest standard. 'I have learnt everything in life except how to live', is the confession Arnold Bennett expressed through a character in one of his novels. The shortage of teachers of Religious Knowledge who are professing Christians is one measure of this need.

How urgent and deep is this need in *the world of science*! I remember saying – what so many must have thought – when I drew my wife's attention to the headline in the morning paper about the dropping of the first atom bomb: 'The world will never be the same again now.' Since 1945, the ancient words have become as with so much more in the Bible, increasingly significant: 'And unto this people thou shalt say, Thus saith the Lord; Behold, I set before you the way of life, and the way of death' (Jeremiah 21.8). Science has no gospel. It continues to reveal the power God has given man over nature to 'subdue it' and the responsibility given to man by the gift of free will and choice (the greatest risk God took in all His creations by His desire to make men in His own image and not robots). The responsibility for what we do with the results of scientific research is collective and personal, and scientists, as with all other men and women, are morally concerned (witness the afterthoughts of some of the scientists whose work led to the fashioning of the 'hell' bomb).

The world of industry needs the Gospel, and this has become increasingly recognized in my life-time by the development of industrial missions and particular training for those accepting this vocation. What a magnificent lead has been given by my friend the Rev. William Gowland at Luton in this mission. Both sides (an unfortunate word if 'taking sides' means opposition and competition rather than co-operation) are in travail for greater harmony and unity; and, as Sir Alfred Owen and others have shown, the nearer one comes to the acceptance of the principles revealed in the teaching of a one-time carpenter at Nazareth, as for example: 'Do unto others as ye would have them do unto you', the more sure are the fruits of happiness, goodwill and true progress ensured. The alternatives are bitterness, suspicion, and strife which impoverish not only industry, but the nation and the world.

It is true also of *the world of politics*. I have never thought of politics as 'a dirty game', but anyone interested who reads political books, especially lives of politicians (including the greatest names in all parties) will realize that there are many more politicians than statesmen, and all are men of like passions to ourselves. Unworthy compromise and intrigue, excessive emphasis on 'the art of the possible' and far too little on 'with God all things are possible', lack of spiritual vision and vigorous moral purpose are not as evident as many would like to see (though more than is commonly supposed) in those who frame our legislation. For my part, I thank God for what I believe is a steady progress in the influence of Christian faith in practice at Westminster. The Welfare State and the most striking developments in the present century of social concern for our fellows are not just indirectly associated with the Christian faith, but the need for more translation of the revolutionary and regenerating truth of the Gospel, in all its implications and applications, is still evident.

Mention of the Welfare State is a reminder of the National Health Service and the wonderful progress in medical science in the twentieth Century, but more of the gospel is needed in *the medical world*. Not least in this increasing progress is the fuller recognition of a patient being more than a case, and maladies more than symptoms. The trinity of the soul, mind and body – the health or wholeness from integration which stems from integrity – is now recognized more generally than ever before. Thus doctors and ministers are finding their way to closer co-operation in providing the conditions in which God, who alone heals, can mediate His power. '*Mens agitat molem*' was the motto of my old College, and a mind in conflict, a guilty conscience, a tormenting anxiety and other inner feelings can produce physical illness. Our hospitals are full of such patients, as statistics show. Such troubles are described by the Psalmist in Psalm 32, resulting in sleeplessness, premature ageing, aching limbs and lack of saliva for proper mastication (a test used in trying to determine guilt in medieval times). Like my dear mother, when faced with a medical crisis, I believe it to be true what she said to the surgeon: 'I believe in medical skill, Doctor, and I believe in prayer.' 'Good for you,' was his reply. We need more of the Gospel in the medical world, both in research and practice.

We need it in the *world of international relations*. 'No man liveth unto himself', says the good old book. Neither does a nation in this modern world where practical isolationism is as dead as Queen Anne. If life is to continue on this planet, we have got to find the way to live together as God intended as a family of His children otherwise the alternative would seem to be international suicide. 'As a biologist I have reached this conclusion: we have come to the turning point in the human habitation of the earth', says Barry Commoner in his book *Science and Survival*. Science in my life-time has turned the world into a neighbourhood but we are not good neighbours, as the stupid, sinful barriers of the various 'walls', colour bar, anti-semitism and the like show. The larger truth of God's purpose for His world is seeking to enter life and men are afraid

15

of it. The truth is that 'God has made of one blood all men for to dwell upon the face of the earth'. It is sanity and wisdom to think and plan in terms of a world as an economic unit. There is no longer any abiding security for any nation or group of nations in armaments. To my grandmother, a war in China was in another world. She was sorry there should be bloodshed there, but it had little, if any, visible effect upon her daily life in Wakefield. Today economists continually demonstrate in various ways the truth of what Paul wrote long years ago: 'Who is weak and I am not weak?' There is only one real hope for men as individuals and mankind as a whole, it is the hope of the Gospel. There is an evangelical message for a world in economic confusion and chaos, in anxiety and fear, in division through affluence and poverty, in waste (over 4,000 millions annually spent on armaments) and want (two-thirds of the population suffering from malnutrition and hunger). The message is 'Seek first the Kingdom of God and His righteousness and all these things shall be added unto you'. All these things, as the context of the passage shows, include food, clothing and physical needs. As an agricultural scientist, I believe God has so made the world that, if rightly used – including the full application of the present known scientific resources – there is enough for all of God's family. We pay but lip service (not always that) to the words inscribed on the Royal Exchange, London, namely: 'The earth is the Lord's and the fullness thereof.' Christians believe we are trustees of material things for God. We could go a long way with our present scientific knowledge (which is always increasing) in realizing 'the fullness thereof' of mother earth, but of what use is increased agricultural production if the channels of distribution are blocked by envy, fear, malice and selfishness or any other form of sin contrary to 'His Righteousness'? We need more of the Gospel in the United (?) Nations and running through all our international relationships.

We need the Gospel in *the world of the space age*. Sir Bernard Lovell, the distinguished scientist, head of Jodrell Bank, has spoken of the possible immoral use of space and of men claiming that space is 'ours' and the fullness thereof. The Gospel, it has been truly said, is cosmic. An indication of the possibility of this increasing use of scientific discovery without regard to God's laws, which are prevalent in all the worlds and the worlds that are to be, is revealed in the Russian astronaut's statement that he found no God in space. Men can repeat in modern form the disaster of the Tower of Babel.

From the world of outer space let us return to the world which is more real to everyman, namely the home. We need the Gospel *in the world of home life*. Does anyone doubt that we would make a vital contribution to the moral and spiritual leadership of Great Britain (infinitely more important than financial or military leadership) by an increase in truly Christian homes? Is there not a connection between the increasing problems of youth and the absence of parental responsibility, discipline and example in the home? Does anyone know of a better safeguard or a finer security for a young life than a Christian, loving upbringing? It is possible that the reader may say: 'What has all this to do with personal evangelism?' The answer surely is 'Everything!' 'All our problems are theological ones', said Archbishop William Temple. If the solution of the world's problems is in the Gospel of Jesus Christ – and the heart of its problems is that of personal relationships – then the worlds within the world I have briefly enumerated can only be permeated by the Gospel through *persons* committed to Christ. Evangelism is only possible through evangelists. We tend too much in these days to use abstract words or words in an abstract sense; for example, world, masses, classes, youth, economics, statistics. Too often figures relating to hunger, poverty or destitution are not *seen* as human faces. To become 'involved in the world' – the much-used slogan in Christian writings today – means essentially with persons, remembering that the Gospel of the Kingdom of God is concerned with men's bodies as well as their souls. The full-orbed Gospel includes the so-called social Gospel, and Christians should be in the van of all who strive and serve to make the world a better place for the girls and boys growing up in our midst. If the question be asked 'What is the relation between individual conversion to God and conversion to His purposes in the world?', the answer is that exemplified in the lives of the first Apostles. Those who won individuals for Christ were those who were described also as 'having turned the world upside down', or as my father put it 'right side up'.

'The benefits of religion are without limit not only for this life but for the life to come', writes Paul to the young Timothy (1 Timothy 4.8). The Church of my early days has been charged – not always I think justly – with being too other-worldly. In these days the pendulum has swung in the other direction. A well-balanced Christian seeks to express God's mission in making known the promise of the best of both worlds of time and eternity, though placing the greater emphasis, as Jesus, who fed the hungry and healed the sick, did on the soul and its eternal welfare. Personal evangelism is making known the whole Gospel for the whole man for the whole world; and because the fullness of the stature of manhood in Christ is so perfect, it is understandable if in our human limitations preaching is often complementary in the variety of emphasis laid upon this or that aspect of the manifold truth of the Gospels. Lord Soper, Dr Billy Graham, Dr Martin Luther King, Dr John Vincent and Dr Martyn Lloyd Jones are examples which immediately come to my mind in this connection. Paul did not preclude judgement of different types of preaching, and whilst in prison heard of preachers who did not preach as he himself did; but I sometimes wish all preachers had his grace of Christian tolerance when he wrote, 'What does it matter? One way or another, in pretence or sincerity Christ is set forth, and for that I rejoice' (Philippians, 1.18, N.E.B.).

The all-important fact I seek to declare is the utter relevance to every man, every situation, every experience, every circumstance, every problem and every need of the glorious splendour of the Gospel. You cannot take it to the wrong person or place.

The Church has many ministries, some of which are now of considerable State concern, though still leaving abundant opportunities for personal service, but it has one mission which is its Christ-given priority. It is 'to make Christians' through personal evangelism. That is the inescapable, though not unavoidable, challenge to every Christian. It is a costly mission, as He who inaugurated this mission on earth knew it would be. It means blood and sweat and tears, and, if need be, sacrificing life itself, now as in every age since Calvary. It involves such patience, forbearance, long-suffering, sharing and loving as only supernatural power and grace can inspire and sustain, hence the essential need of union with the Living Christ whose work is still 'to seek and to save that which is lost'.

Difficult and arduous as the task of personal evangelism is – and not without its peculiar perils to the evangelist himself, – it is nevertheless the way of the highest joy in the service of Christ. 'That my joy might remain in you and that your joy might be full' (John 15.11), was His desire and therefore prayer for His disciples. What was His joy? Unquestionably that of doing the Father's will and in particular the bringing home to God those who were estranged from Him, those who were lost until He found them. Read again the unforgettable stories in Luke's Gospel, chapter 15, of the lost sheep, the lost coin and the lost son, and in each case note the joy on finding. 'Likewise there is joy in the presence of the angels of God over one sinner that repenteth.' This is without doubt *the* joy of the Lord of heaven and earth. Is it then conceivable that this joy should be denied to any one of His true disciples? This book would never have been attempted were it not for the life-long conviction that *every Christian* can be a link in the chain of personal evangelism and therefore share in the joy of Christ.

'If anybody had said to me: "Somebody has left you twenty thousand pounds", I should not have given a snap of my fingers for it, compared with the joy which I felt when I was told God had saved a soul through my ministry.' Thus spoke Charles Haddon Spurgeon, the world-famed London preacher. I suppose that would have meant over £60,000 or more today. 'I cannot tell you what joy it gave me to bring the first soul to the Lord Jesus Christ. I have tasted almost all the pleasures that this world can give. I do not suppose there is one that I have not experienced, but I can tell you that those pleasures were as nothing compared to the joy that the saving of the soul gave me.' Thus spoke C. T. Studd, one-time Cambridge Blue and England Test Cricketer.

It is the same incomparable joy which my friend Dr Leslie Weatherhead meant when, in speaking on 'Jesus and Young Men' and referring to the ministry as a vocation, he said: 'And if ever you see a life that was travelling along a wrong road suddenly halted by Christ and through words of yours directed along another road known to be the road of God's plan, then, my dear fellow, you will not be able to sleep for happiness.' I have proved his words to be true.

The most important decision we have to make in life is in answer to the question Pilate asked when confronted with Jesus; 'What shall I do, then, with Jesus, which is called Christ?' If, in an encounter with Him, I respond in loving obedience to His call, I become a Christian, but this answer then involves other questions. This is to be expected, for it applies to every vocation. A young man leaving school decides he wants to be a doctor. This is a major decision, but at once it raises questions as to entry to a medical school, lodgings, text books, timetable of lectures, equipment and finance, and so on. The Christian, having given his life to Christ, is faced with several questions, one of which is: 'What kind of a Christian am I going to be?' There are Christians and Christians, as are described in the New Testament. John Wesley described two kinds – the good and the best. Not all Christians are actively engaged in the mission expressed in personal evangelism. Their personal witness for Christ in everyday life is seldom, if ever, vocal. Years ago, I remember Dr W. E. Sangster and me going over one of his manuscripts for publication as a booklet and making the suggestion that the addition of a few questions at the end might further its use in fellowship groups. Amongst the questions ultimately decided upon in our conversation was this one: 'Could you lead another soul to Christ? When did you last try?' This is a challenge every Christian should face regularly in the presence of Him who commanded His disciples to 'go and make Christians'. It cannot be said too often, and will certainly be repeated in these pages, that to do so we must know Christ for ourselves and have found at His Cross a personal experience of His redeeming grace.

I was once invited to preach at Halton Lea Gate and was uncertain about how to get there. I asked one man a few weeks before the appointed Sunday, and his reply was: 'I've heard of it, but I've never been there, so I'm afraid I can't help you.' Later I put my question to another friend, who replied: 'Halton Lea Gate? Yes, it is somewhere south of Haltwhistle, up the Tyne Valley, but I couldn't say whether it is in Northumberland or Cumberland. In any case, it's so long since I was there, I couldn't be sure.' I had to preach in the morning of that day at Haltwhistle, and in my congregation I was glad to see a dear friend, a former member of my own weekly Fellowship Group, now living in that area. At the end of the service, I greeted him and said: 'Billy, you're just the man to help me. Which is the best road to Halton Lea Gate?' 'Yes, I can help you. I go there regularly, and what's more I am going to the evening service and will take you with me.' Substitute Calvary for Halton Lea Gate, and you will know the challenge of the illustration. A personal evangelist knows he has been there – many times – and he has first-hand knowledge of its saving power and can say to a seeking, troubled soul: 'I'll go with you.'

God's mission through you and me is to bring men and women to believe the good news of the Gospel and to know that *not to believe*, having heard the Gospel, is to sin against the light, the light of the Holy Spirit. For this indeed is the sin of all sins – the deadly sin – which Jesus declared the Holy Spirit would expose, for 'He will convict them of wrong, by their refusal to believe in me' (John 16.9, N.E.B.). Not to believe in Christ – and therefore in all He Himself believed, and will enable all who trust in Him to believe – is to be lost. The best known New Testament verse is John 3. 16. God's message of love in Christ and gift of everlasting life to *whosoever* believeth in Christ. To choose to ignore, reject or neglect this offer is to perish. Truly the Gospel is a matter of life and death, hence the urgency and earnestness which should characterize all who proclaim it.

If one of our kith and kin was in danger of losing his life, would we not do all in our power to save him? Remember Saul Kane's testimony after his Christian conversion: 'I knew that Christ had given me birth to brother all the souls on earth' (*The Everlasting Mercy*, by John Masefield), and we do that in the best way when we bring them to Christ, our Elder Brother.

Well, then, Christians are all called to be actively engaged in mission, *the* mission of winning men and women for Christ in every part of *their* world. Mrs Margaret Knight said to a friend of mine that it was her ambition to speak to as many young university students as possible to *dissuade* them from believing the Christian faith! What am I doing to persuade them? I understand that every member of the Jehovah's

Witnesses must give at least a hundred hours a month to canvassing for their faith. Door to door, person to person, is their method, the same as is regarded in political elections to be the most effective means of winning votes. The commission of Christ was to individuals to go forth and win individuals; for all evangelism, in the final analysis, is personal evangelism.

I have stressed in this opening chapter the worlds within the world in which our mission as personal evangelists is to be expressed, because I cannot over-emphasize the importance of every Christian thinking, like Wesley, that 'the world is my parish' – the world, that is, of *persons*. Put in other words, it means the world of my home, my business, my social and private life, my friends, my associates, my usual and my new contacts with people. Personal evangelism is not an organized campaign, though it can include that, but a life witnessing to the Gospel in all circumstances. The most needed place for such witness, especially with our lips, is not inside the church. It is not usually very difficult to get people to give addresses or engage in discussion of Christian topics within the church, yet the same people may be silent in the world outside concerning their faith in Christ. 'The field is the world', said Jesus, and that is where He calls us to sow the seed of the Gospel and keep on sowing it. And the sower is a person. 'We can preach the Gospel to masses, but men must be saved one by one', writes Canon Bryan Green in *The Practice of Evangelism*. Moreover, in this work, we are called to be both sowers and reapers, for Jesus calls His disciples to both activities. 'Others have laboured and ye have entered into their labours.' And again: 'The harvest is plenteous, but the labourers are few: pray ye therefore the Lord of the harvest, that he send forth labourers into his harvest.' You couldn't pray such a prayer and withhold your personal labour – or could you? The priesthood of all believers is a belief which carries personal, practical application through the church *in the world*. To go to God on behalf of the people and then to the people on behalf of God is this priestly function. Wherever, then, in the world the Christian finds himself with non-Christians – which means the majority of people he meets in daily life who are uncommitted to Christ – he is called to be a priest unto God and for God. His church work – so called – is but a preparation, inspiration and source of power – for the outreaching work of the church beyond its walls. He is not of this world but he is in it, to make the Saviour of the World known and real to *persons*.

CHAPTER TWO

THE MEANING

'He first findeth his own brother, Simon. . . . And he brought him to Jesus'. (John 1.41–42, A.V.)

WHAT IS evangelism? It has been said that the World Council Churches cannot agree on a definition. For my part, all my life I have believed it meant the bringing of a man or woman to a personal commitment to Christ in response to the offer of the Gospel, *and Christ is the Gospel.* That implies preaching the Gospel, and in doing so seeking for a definite response. It is bringing Christ to people and people to Christ. There are different forms of evangelism: e.g., mass evangelism, but in the end it is always personal evangelism – person to person. It means becoming by His promise a fisher for men, 'but fishing with the line.' A personal call, leading to a personal decision to accept a personal Saviour makes possible a personal knowledge and experience of Christ. 'I offered them Christ', wrote John Wesley in his Journal. 'O let me commend my Saviour to you', wrote his brother Charles in one of his hymns – note the personal pronouns. This is the function of the Church through the teaching and preaching of the Gospel in the Church and Sunday School, in the home and in the world, through both corporate and individual witness. All Christians are called to be personal evangelists, that through human lips and lives the Gospel may reach individual lives.

Beginning as did Andrew with his own brother, Simon, this is incontrovertibly the method by which the Christian faith from its first days spread so rapidly throughout the world. In its beginning, the Christian Church was subjected to intense persecution, which included the martyrdom of Stephen, and as Luke tells us in Acts 8.1, the disciples 'were all scattered abroad', but God's purpose is not defeated by the sin and folly of men, for a few verses later we read: 'Therefore they that were scattered abroad went everywhere preaching the word.' It is important to note two things from the same chapter: (1) Many were ordinary, unnamed persons, for the first known apostles or leaders of the Church remained at the beginning in Jerusalem (v. 14) and (2) it was personal evangelism as evidenced by the winning for Christ of Simon the sorcerer in the city of Samaria, and of the Ethiopian by the roadside as Philip 'told him the good news of Jesus' (Acts 8.35, R.S.V.).

Every large movement has grown by the same method, to cite only four examples: Socialism, Methodism, the Salvation Army, Communism. The crises of every century are concerned with the major conflict between the kingdom of God and the kingdom of evil, between what Jesus called light and darkness. God has chosen to reveal His power to redeem the world of men and women through personal lives and personal testimony, and personal evangelists are those who continue faithfully, saying so, more persuasively, more precisely and more personally every day. There is an intimacy, an immediacy and an impact made in personal evangelism that especially belong to this form of evangelism. It is significant that in the Gospel records of the New Testament – all that we possess of the teaching and life of Jesus in the days of his life on earth – there are details of nineteen personal interviews which He has with men and women. Unlike a minister who was described to me as one who, when he talks to you personally, always seems as if he wants to move on, Jesus always had time for an individual, giving up most of a day, for example to Zaccheus, and part of a night to Nicodemus. In the light of our supreme Example, consider what it means to engage in personal evangelism.

1. Consecration of Time

'Follow me and I will make you fishers of men.' No one would describe fishing as a speedy business or something one can accomplish in a hurry. For over thirty years I have been led to reserve Saturday evenings for personal interviews with men and women in my own home, concerning moral and spiritual problems. For a similar period of time, as stated in my preface, I have been privileged to lead my present weekly Men's Fellowship which, amongst other things, has been used directly and indirectly to introduce people to Christ, and a not uncommon enquiry sometimes after a few weeks' attendance has been: 'When may I have a private talk with you?' to which the reply is 'Saturday night after six if convenient to you, but if not I'll do my best to fix up another day and time to suit you'. Obviously, like any other layman or minister adopting the same method in being available for spiritual counselling, one could have used the time for other purposes, but I cannot begin to tell how much I have received by blocking in, in every diary, this night of each week for both receiving and sharing God's blessings. Every one must come to terms with time, even as Jesus did, for as He put it: 'I must work the works of Him that hath sent me while it is day: the night cometh, when no man can work.' Every day is a gift of God of time and should begin with the prayer: 'Lord, what wilt Thou have me to do?' Much of the day will be taken up by fulfilling the responsibilities laid upon me by service through work in order to earn a necessary livelihood – and this, too, I should always regard as a most important sphere for personal evangelism, both consciously and unconsciously, for the personal evangelist must shine for Christ in and at his daily work. There remain other hours in the week when I have alternative choice of how I shall spend (invest) my time. Many good causes – more than ever in these days – offer opportunities for service, and recreation also is a necessary part of a Christian's time-table to enable re-creation for service. The question which should be faced regularly is not what is a good way of using the precious gift of time, but what is God's best way for me. Of Professor Henry Drummond, the great Edinburgh evangelist, the Rev. Tom Dring writes, 'Drummond declined innumerable invitations to address crowded meetings that he might give himself to personal work, mostly among students'.

How true it is that the enemy of the best is the good. 'Take time to be holy, speak oft with thy Lord.' Without such time spent in communion in prayer, the study of God's Word, the use of the means of grace (especially of public worship and of a regular Christian fellowship group), we cannot hope to be spiritual counsellors whom God can use as personal evangelists. All this means time, to which must be added the time spent in 'seeking and finding the lost'.

Did not Ruskin say: 'If I read this, I cannot read that', which may be interpreted not only as an exhortation to choose the best, but as a reminder that you haven't time for everything. Personal evangelism is a full-time job in the sense that at work and at play, in the home and in the church and in the whole world of my personal activities and contacts, I have faith to proclaim, a message to convey, a way of life to offer, which pervades my whole being. It was said of an American multi-millionaire that 'he had a religion, but he kept it in sacred detachment from his business'. What a travesty of the Christian faith, and how utterly remote from personal evangelism! The mistake so many of us make is to live our life in compartments, and to talk of church work and daily work, of sacred and secular. The church's greatest work should be done when its members are engaged in their daily work; there is nothing in a Christian's life which cannot be done to the glory of God in the hope and prayer that in so doing men may come to glorify God. (If our job does seem directly to involve us in the devil's work, we ought to ask God to enable us to change it.) This does not mean that we rely entirely on the silent witness to our faith, though clearly if our personal life is not an interpretation or illustration of what we say with our lips we had better be silent. It means that we seize every opportunity – how many there are if we are alive to them – of using conversation to the glory of God. 'Let the redeemed of the Lord say so.' 'They shall speak of the glory of Thy Kingdom', writes the Psalmist. Even more searching and challenging to us modern Christians is Paul's sequence of questions in Romans 10. In 14 and 15, following his affirmation 'Whosoever shall call upon the name of the Lord shall be saved'. 'Now how

can they call on one in whom they have never believed?'
'How can they believe in one of whom they have never
heard, and how can they hear unless some one proclaim
him?' 'And who will go to tell them unless he is sent?'
(Phillips translation.)

It takes time to commune with God and time to
communicate the Gospel to others, for in both cases
it must not be a monologue, but a dialogue and always
a willingness to listen as well as to speak. We have to
learn to *wait* upon God for *His* word of guidance and
blessing. *In Spiritual counselling we must encourage the*
person to talk and wait with patience for the revealing moment
when the Holy Spirit seeks our co-operation in speech.

I remember seeing an analysis of the subjects in
ordinary daily conversation which gave the following
for men:

Business – 25 per cent of time.
Sporting activities – 20 per cent.
Daily news – 15 per cent.
Family affairs – 10 per cent.
Social activities – 10 per cent.
Investments, bets, etc. – 10 per cent.
Anecdotes and jokes – 5 per cent.

Religion as such was never mentioned, though 5 per
cent remained for cultural subjects. In women, 30 per
cent was given to domestic affairs, 20 per cent for social
activities, 20 per cent for dress and household activities
15 per cent for local news and so on. Miss Rita Snowden
writes of an instrument developed by Professor Oldfield
of Oxford, a miniature microphone for recording all
one says throughout the day. It was a challenge to me
to consider my own daily conversation.

Beginning then with contacts in our daily life, sometimes through favours done or asked for, though mainly through natural, friendly conversation, we become interested in people and interest continued begets knowledge. Clearly we need the guidance of the Holy Spirit in deciding whether and how He desires us to follow up the contact made in conversation because of interest shown, questions asked, a need shared, a conscience quickened, a desire to know more expressed. The next discussion is usually best carried out in your own home or that of the friend you have made in the contact, sometimes resulting from several brief conversations you may have had with the person for whom you have a God-given concern. Such conversations with the same person may extend over weeks, months and, in some cases, years. Letters may be exchanged, and, whilst the personal evangelist must guard against becoming an unwanted friend in this particular matter, he should never cease his efforts until he senses and confirms by friendly enquiry that further discussion of any kind on the subject is not desired. Even then, prayer need not cease. I once prayed for a man who left my Fellowship in Newcastle to go and seek for employment in London. He agreed in our last conversation together that he had not found the experience I desired so much for him of a personal experience of Christ as Saviour and Lord, though he readily admitted that he had realized its validity by attendance at our meetings, and wished at times he possessed it. I promised I would pray for him that in God's own way and time what he had seen in others might become his own possession. I also promised I would write to him once a month, but if ever he desired me to give up writing, all he need do was not to reply. For some months we exchanged letters, then, after two letters from me with no reply, I made clear in the second letter that I would continue to pray regularly for him, and whenever he wanted to hear from me all that was required was a post-card or letter from him. For six years I prayed daily and heard nothing. Then one day my mail contained a letter from Dr W. E. Sangster who, after preaching the previous Sunday evening at the Central Hall, Westminster (where he ministered for sixteen years), wrote to say he had felt led to make an appeal for decision for Christ. Amongst those who responded and subsequently met him in his vestry after the service for prayer and counsel was a man who, he believed, was truly converted that night. He had been a non-churchgoer for some years and had wandered in a spiritual wilderness. The first thing he asked Dr Sangster to do when he rose from his knees was to write and tell me that he had now found the real experience of Christ – *he was my man*, and my prayers were abundantly answered. Wisely, Dr Sangster put him to work for the Master as soon as possible, and his first responsibility was in connection with a team whose privilege it was to make a friendly contact with any visitors, in the 2,000 and more congregation, who were coloured people, and make them welcome. Later he became Society Steward (often quoted by Dr Sangster as a model one) at one of the churches in the Westminster Circuit, and still later a fully accredited Methodist local preacher.

All this illustrates – and so much will be added – that provision of time is *vital*. A personal evangelist has to decide what shall have priority in his use of it, and this must be a weekly, and often daily, prayer*ful* consideration.

2. Consecration of Experience

Like the medical practitioner who gains experience which can be used to such benefit for others as the years pass, so the personal evangelist increases his knowledge of human nature and experience in dealing with men and women by the consecrated practice of evangelism. Whilst, no two persons are exactly alike, needs and distresses have a certain resemblance and all who have not accepted Christ are by nature in need of the Saviour. Professor C. Kingsley Barrett (Durham University) in his wonderful little book, *Reading through Romans*, writes: 'The root of the matter is that God has only one way of dealing with men – in mercy; and to this in one way or another they must be brought. . . . Whatever sort of person I am: gross sinner; busy Church worker; untaught child; trained scholar – whatever I am, if I am to know God at all I must know Him as the merciful God.' How true! For the offer of forgiveness is the heart of the Gospel and the Saviour's prayer on His Cross, the prayer for all men.

All my experience, then, firstly of Christ's saving work in my own soul, secondly, without breaking the strict confidence won and reposed in me by previous enquirers the knowledge of what He has done in other lives, and thirdly and supremely the knowledge that Christ can make a Christian of anybody and everybody – all this experience can be blessed of the Holy Spirit and will be confirmed and enriched the longer you remain faithful to His call to be an evangelist. So we are able to say what He has done for me He can do for you, what He is to others He can be to you, if only you are willing to accept His will and way in your life without conditions. In all our conversation, however, Christ must have the pre-eminence. Talk of yourself must be entirely subordinate to talk about Him. 'Looking unto Jesus, the author and finisher of our faith' should be our constant aim and implied invitation to the person you are seeking to win for Christ. Argument has its place, dialogue can be used of the Holy Spirit, but bear in mind that some people love *just to argue*, have no intention of doing more than argue and can hide behind a smoke-screen of discussion their moral and spiritual need. Honest doubt should be patiently listened to and honestly appreciated. Experience will enable the spiritual counsellor to know when to guide the conversation back to the personal challenge of the Gospel and the same experience – all of the Holy Spirit's giving – to determine if and when an appeal for personal acceptance is to be made. I have known the latter moment to be after one interview of an hour or two or less. On another occasion, after a Saturday night interview, a young man went home, had a sleepless night and returned to my home at 8 a.m. on a Sunday morning to make a complete surrender of his life to Christ in my presence as a praying witness. To have pressed for a decision a few hours earlier would have been wrong. In another example I felt guided to say after a talk: 'Will you make me a promise?' 'Not until I know what it is', was the wise reply, to which I made response in these words: 'I am sure you are not far from the Kingdom. I am sure, too, that you will never find the happiness and zest you seek for until you make up your mind. At present you are trying to get the best of both worlds and failing *miserably*. Promise that when you hear His call, and if you ask to hear it and mean it, you will; that at that moment you will do *exactly* what He asks you to do. That is the promise.' 'I will promise that', she said.

Above my mantelpiece I have a picture of Jesus walking through the cornfield with some of His first disciples – a picture of His wonderful group fellowship, walking and talking with Jesus. Alongside it, on a small card printed in bold letters, are words I received in a wonderful way: **ASK HIM** – these words so often act as the invitation to enquirers and counsellor alike after discussion, argument and conversation. So we knelt that night in my little room to ask God to enable the promise to be kept – that and nothing more. A week later my phone rang. It was a message from the enquirer, who wanted to see me that I might hear of the decision made to go forward at a Billy Graham sound relay service in response to the appeal in Brunswick Methodist Church, Newcastle upon Tyne. I had not been responsible for the invitation to go to the service, but the promise made the previous Saturday had been kept. God needed Billy Graham as well as Cecil Pawson to win that young and gifted university student. Which gives me the opportunity to say that whenever I see anyone making a decision for Christ, whether at the close of a public service I have been privileged to conduct or in the privacy of my own or another's home, I always thank God for the prayers, teaching, preaching, love and messages of lips and lives of so many who have been used of God to bring this life to this decision making possible conversion or re-dedication. It is because of this truth of experience that one of my deep convictions is that every Christian can be used of God to bring others to Christ. We shall reap where others have sown and sow for others to reap as well as sow in unproductive conditions (*vide* the parable of the Sower).

3. Consecration of Oneself

Personal evangelism means for the personal evangelist the giving of one's whole self to Christ. We cannot hope to be used by God to convert others unless we ourselves are converted. Only when we know Him for ourselves can we make Him known to others, and as we know Him better, we shall make Him better known. When King David made his great appeal to his people, having first made known his own gift, for the building of the temple, he ended by saying: 'And who then is willing to consecrate his service this day unto the Lord?' (1 Chronicles 29.5). That is the Authorised Version. The Revised Version has a significant change which for me became an enriching, personal challenge. It is: 'Who then offereth willingly to consecrate himself this day unto the Lord?' 'Consecrating himself' is the translation of the R.S.V., but whatever the meaning of the original text (Hebrew: 'to fill his hand') the truth is, as I know from experience, that it is possible to give a lot to God without giving yourself, to continue in His service and over the years take back part of what you once gave to Him, or, most subtle temptation of all, to keep back part of your life which He wants to possess wholly. Evelyn Underhill once wrote of some people who 'desert Christ and enter His service instead'. It is certain that we can never be personal evangelists if we keep back any part of ourselves from Him. I wonder if this unwillingness to become involved in the costly time-consuming and energy-expending work of personal evangelism is the cause of the present-day scarcity of personal witness and personal evangelism in an active sense amongst so many members in all the churches of today. A great saint of God once confessed that for years he had kept back one room of the house of his soul from Christ. The day came when he handed over the key to this room and gave his Lord full access and control of his whole life. From that moment he said he knew a new sense of power to witness, a new experience of fruitfulness in discipleship, a new sense of joy and peace he had never experienced hitherto.

Let me count the cost of such dedication to Christ and His work of evangelism, but also count the cost of missing all the blessings both here and hereafter which acceptance of it brings. It means heartbreak at times, disappointments, failures and always a sharing of His travail for the souls of men and women. Jesus had his backsliders, 'From that time many of His disciples went back, and walked no more with Him' (John 6.66). A significant word is 'disciples', not the curious, the interested or uncommitted, but those who had professed in some measure to be His followers. What pathos lies in the words of Jesus as He turned at that moment to twelve men and said: 'Will ye also go away?' Yes, you will have your disappointments and failures. John Wesley knew many, yet so hoped and prayed for their return that in his original hymn-book he had two whole sections devoted to them. But there is one other word about the meaning of personal evangelism which must be said, and I shall return to it again and again and end with it. That is that you will share the Master's joy, if in this glorious work you continue to be faithful.

In Peter Parson's Log in the *British Weekly* for June 22nd, 1967, there appeared this paragraph for one of the days of the week: 'In view of such biblical sayings as 'In His presence there is fullness of joy' and 'Enter thou into the joy of thy Lord' may we not say that the purpose of living is to enjoy oneself? Yet the moment one puts it as starkly as that, reaction sets in. Duty, discipline, sacrifice, rigour; how much more at home we are with these concepts.' I see his point and to so many religion is a duty, not a delight, austerity without joy, drab and not persuasively attractive. Such is always a travesty of the real Christian experience and certainly that of the personal evangelist. C. S. Lewis, in his book *The Problem of Pain*, began as follows: 'Not many years ago when I was an atheist . . .' The story of his conversion he entitled *Surprised by Joy*. It is truly a 'happy day that fixed my choice on Thee my Saviour and my Lord' and it becomes increasingly so as we live to bring others into that limitless experience of happiness. For 'holiness is happiness', as John Wesley affirmed.

Let Billy Bray, the Cornish miner and great personal evangelist, speak for all like him who, having come to know Christ, from then onwards live to make Him known. 'I was a new man altogether. I told all I met what the Lord had done for my soul. I have heard some say they have had hard work to get away from their companions but I sought mine out and had hard work to find them soon enough to tell them what the Lord had done for me. Some said I was mad; and others that they should get me back again next pay day. But praise the Lord it is now more than forty years and they have not got me yet. They said I was a *mad*-man, but they meant I was a *glad*-man, and glory be to God! I have been glad ever since' (see *Billy Bray*, by F. W. Bourne, page 11).

CHAPTER THREE

THE MESSAGE

'It is in him that you reach your full life'
(Colossians 2.10, Moffatt's translation).

THE APPROACH to the message of the personal
evangelist will vary as persons are varied, but the heart
of the evangel will be the same. I was once asked in a
meeting of students: 'What do you miss if you do not
become a Christian?' I answered by saying, 'I wish I
had an hour or more to make reply, but in one word
the answer is *Life*'. Given a good digestion, ample
financial resources, a pleasant occupation, variety of
interests, one may experience a pleasurable existence,
but real life is something more than a measure of
personal happiness and comfort or achievement and
attainment limited to years of time. The heart of the
Gospel is that God, 'Whose will it is that all men should
find salvation, and come to know the truth' (1 Timothy
2.4, N.E.B.), loves each one of us personally and desires
for each of His children fulfilment of our life here in
His eternal fellowship. For that unique purpose He
sent and gave His Son to this world 'that whosoever
believeth in him should not perish but have everlasting
life'. (John 3.16). That is the truth about God, about
life, about ourselves and about what we may become
through Him who is 'the Way, the Truth and the
Life'. Jesus declared the reason for His life here on

earth with unmistakable meaning when He said: 'I am come that they might have life and that they might have it more abundantly' (John 10.10). The New Testament confirms this truth again and again – of the gift of new life in Christ – and never more plainly than in these words:

'And this is the record, that God hath given to us eternal life and this life is in his Son.

He that hath the Son hath life; and he that hath not the Son of God hath not life' (1 John 5, 11 and 12).

It was a man who appeared to have everything that men today believe provides satisfaction who came to Jesus and said: 'What lack I yet?' He had great material possessions, high moral standards, social prestige and power but he recognized Jesus had life – and real life always has an eternal quality – whereas he, by comparison, felt incomplete. That he knew he was missing real life accounted for his partial answer to his own question when he said: 'Good Master, what shall I do that I may inherit eternal life?' Well, we do not inherit it – it is a gift.

Personal evangelism is therefore the offer of a new nature which results in fullness of life through our Lord Jesus Christ. 'If any man is in Christ he is a new creature.' In Christ means Christ in us. We enter into the eternal world whilst continuing to participate in the everyday life of this world. He is born again, which Jesus insisted is a 'must' if he is to see and know the Kingdom, Created in the flesh, he is re-created by the Spirit – in a word, made all over again. 'All I can say,' said his coachman, 'is that though there's the same skin, there's a new man inside.' This was said of Studd and quoted by I. C. Pollock in his book, *Moody without Sankey*. Conversion, which means change, is an apt description, and this is the work of the Holy Spirit within the soul. (Opposite to my home is a house which was given a 'face lift', but the important changes were internal when it was *converted* into flats.) Personal commitment makes possible this re-creation, for without my assent, no power in earth or heaven can make me a Christian. The appeal of the evangelist is therefore for a personal decision. Yet all is of God, for though I may sing with gratitude and gladness: 'O happy day that fixed *my* choice on Thee, my Saviour and my God', I also sing in the same hymn: 'He drew me and I followed on.' Thus Jesus reminded His first disciples: 'You have not chosen me but I have chosen *you*.'

That human nature needs to be changed ought to be a self-evident fact, especially as we survey the state of the world today and listen to the news. We shall not be judged of God because of the possession of a nature which runs so easily to self and sin (from earliest days of self-consciousness) for we were born with it. This is the judgement that being offered a new nature in Christ we refuse it or 'neglect so great a salvation'. To say we don't need it is tantamount to saying our life is as good as Jesus Christ.

The Bible declares we have all sinned because we have come short of God's dream and desire for us – as seen in the life of perfect obedience to His will in Jesus Christ – and at times every man's conscience secretly, if not openly, agrees. The dilemma of the human heart has never been more clearly described than in Paul's account of the inner conflict between the desire for good and the surrender to evil. 'The good I would I do not and the evil I would not that I do.' The words are sometimes so familiar that their cutting edge becomes blunted. I often use Moffatt's translation: 'The wish is there but not the power of doing what is right.' In all my personal, weekly interviews with all sorts and conditions of men and women in my own home, I have never met one who, when I received his confidence as a friend simply desiring to help, said that this truth was quite irrelevant to them. 'I have always lived up to my highest ideals, have never acted or told a lie, have never been selfish or self-seeking, have never harboured envious or resentful feelings, have never indulged in impure imagination (which Jesus declared can *become* equivalent to an act of adultery) have never lost my temper or wronged in thought, word or deed another person.' Who anywhere would make such a claim? If one did, the charge of God's Word is that one is a liar. 'If we say that we have no sin we deceive ourselves' – ourselves not others, and certainly not God – 'and the truth is not in us'; *but* 'if we confess our sins he is faithful and just to forgive us our sins and to cleanse us from all unrighteousness' (1 John 1.8 and 9).

Conversion begins in the conscious act of turning to God in repentance for all we have done which has grieved Him in our unconverted condition the consequences of which we can never atone for or erase. In a recent biography of John Henry Newman, the writer says of him at fifteen years of age: 'He was turned right round, converted to God.' The new birth – the gift of God – is the work of the Holy Spirit and is marked by the inner consciousness of the presence within of Christ. Just as we were unconscious of our physical birth, so we may not know the exact time or place where we were born again, but in due course we know that we are alive, 'Alive in Him, my living Head', as Charles Wesley puts it in one of his hymns.

But there is life in the womb before actual birth.

John Henry Newman thought the particular movement of the Spirit was present for five months before he was 'turned right round, converted to God'. Sudden conversion is not always as sudden as it appears, not excepting that of Saul, though for him it would seem more so than that of Peter. The uniting bond between all converted persons is the knowledge that it has definitely happened. It is a turning *from* self and idols we have worshipped and served and a turning *to* the worship and service of God. 'From darkness to light...' from the power of Satan to God, as Acts 26.18 declares, which verse I hold contains the Charter of the Church and the meaning of evangelism and conversion. It is God who gives us the power to respond to His will and to accept salvation through Jesus Christ. Regeneration then, or the new birth, is the gift of God through the Holy Spirit, and conversion our change of mind and heart by the power of the same Spirit.

It is hardly credible that we should not know that we have passed from death to life, darkness to light, bondage to liberty, especially when resting our sole assurance and trust not in ourselves, but in God, we experience the promise: 'The Spirit himself beareth witness with our spirit that we are the children of God' (Romans 8.16, R.V.). What my father, a Methodist minister, described as being 'soundly converted' implied an act of the whole man, mind and heart, emotion and will, soul and body. As I often put it, we bring the past to be forgiven, the present to be strengthened, the future to be guided, that is we hand over all our life without conditions and qualifications to be re-made 'in Christ' (which means Christ in us). There is no stereotyped form of conversion, yet it may be said that Christ never becomes real to us except out of a sense of need and a personal response to that love more clearly revealed on the Cross than anywhere else – that love which will never let us go, never let us off, and never let us down. This new life brings a deep joyful experience of God in Christ, a new way of looking at life, a new sense of values, a new desire to share 'the good things of the Gospel' with others inside the Christian community of the Church and outside it with those not yet Christian.

I often recall to myself with renewed gratitude and to others I seek to win for Christ the blessings Christ brings to us by looking at my right hand. The first finger symbolises the gift of Pardon (call it forgiveness if preferred, the unique and primary gift of God's reconciling love in Christ); the second finger, 'Peace, which passeth all understanding' when we are made right with God; the third Purpose – that most worthwhile purpose to do God's will; and the last finger, Power – by which to overcome temptation and to accomplish the positive good of His purpose for us. Finally the thumb as signifying the blessing which enables all the foregoing possessions, namely the Presence of Christ within to keep and to hold us with the right hand of His Abiding Companionship. All these are a gift of grace, and it takes two to make complete a gift, one to give and one to receive. 'But as many as received him, to them gave he power to become the sons of God, even to them that believe on his Name.' 'Which were born, not of blood, nor of the will of the flesh, nor of the will of man, but of God.' (John 1.12,13). Come, become and overcome are the blessed words of invitation and promise. If we truly come trusting in Him, in *Christ alone*, as John Wesley said of his experience, we can be assured that 'He

whose word cannot be broken' will save us *from* sin, self
and spiritual death and save us *to* life and holiness and
eternal fellowship with God. The message is, therefore,
life 'in all its fulness' (N.E.B.), 'the shining possibilities
of the life that is eternal' (2 Timothy 1.10, Phillips); it
is ever timely and timeless, 'for in this fellowship has
the Eternal fixed the blessing of an eternal life' (Psalm
133.3, Moffatt).

It is a message for youth with all the promise of the
years ahead. When I was a boy, we often had visiting
preachers and speakers staying in the manse which was
my home. Time and time again, when we boys were
introduced to the visitor, sooner or later the question
would be put: 'When you grow up, what are you going
to be?' Of course, they really meant 'What are you
going to do with your life?' Hence my first ambition
(a lingering trace remains to this day!) to be an engine
driver, next to be a house painter (this latter was short
lived because of my mother's severe discipline after
being discovered practising with paint and brush on
the outside of a window of the house). The time came
when the words were given their true meaning and in
my heart I affirmed, as all young people do at one
time or another: 'To be the best that I can be.' This
is the God-given instinct to live one's life to the full,
one's own life. Many things which contribute to my
life are chosen for me – parents, home, age in which I
was born, colour of my skin, early education. 'Three
things make a man', says Sir Campbell Stuart in his
book *Opportunity Knocks Once*, 'heredity, environment,
temperament.' I do not deny the importance of these
three factors. In my blood-stream and yours runs the
influence of countless ages; to use the Bible description:
'As in Adam *all* . . .'   Robert Louis Stevenson used to

speculate on how much of his grandfather came through his pen as he wrote his essays and stories and how much was 'R. L. S.'. In the popular television series 'Dixon of Dock Green', one title was: 'Like Father like Son'. Yet Campbell Stuart's dictum is only half the truth and therefore can be as dangerous as an untruth, for every man knows the truth of John Oxenham's words:

> 'To every man there openeth
> A high way and a low
> And every man decideth
> The way his soul shall go.'

The vital choice is mine and when confronted by Him who said, 'I am the Way, the Truth and the Life', I know that He speaks these words to me just as surely as He spoke them to Peter, James and John and the other disciples. A normal young person may have many ambitions but he or she can never realize the finest life without the grace of our Lord and Saviour, Jesus Christ. No university education, influential friends, financial resources, intellectual and other gifts can make possible that finest expression of life found in obedience to the call of Him who said to young men, 'Follow me and I will make you . . .' Not self-made, but Christ-made is the secret of a truly successful life. True it is a costly life to live for Christ. Our Lord never concealed the cost, but on the contrary encouraged us to face it. It is well to remember in so doing the cost of rejecting His call and, therefore, of missing the greatest opportunity of time and eternity.

The life that Christ offers enables the *richest possible personality*. The fullest expression of self, paradoxical as it may sound, comes from complete self surrender.

47

'I live,' wrote Paul, 'yet not I, but Christ liveth in me.' For when Christ resolves the inner conflict (which is quite beyond my power to overcome) and cleanses from the guilt and power of sin, He enables me to realize my best potential. Set free to do God's will, God is able to work through all (nothing left out) things for my highest good. I know then what is best and have one unifying purpose, an over-mastering ambition, an absorbing passion 'to press towards the mark of the prize of the high calling in Christ Jesus'. Nothing in the world and in these years of time is so wonderful as to find yourself by losing yourself in Christ.

> *To be the best that I can be*
> *For truth and righteousness and Thee,*
> *Lord of my life, I come.*

To make this choice is not a change for the better but for the best. Blessed indeed is the girl or boy, young man or maiden who coming to Christ finds the answer to the Psalmist's prayer: 'O satisfy us early with thy mercy that we may be glad and rejoice all our days.'

It is life also which enables the *richest possible service.* The instinct to serve is found in many youthful hearts as evidenced by so many youth projects at home and abroad which are for the sake of others. Service in His Name and for Christ's sake and the Gospel's has always an eternal quality even though it be but the giving of a cup of cold water. It was Jesus who made it abundantly clear that our neighbour was anyone anywhere in need to whom we could minister, that in serving even the least and lowest we were doing it to Him, and that to love God and your neighbour as yourself is to know life. At the end of the day – each day and our last day here – that we have done all things 'In Thy Name' and 'For Thy Sake' is to know an inner joy and peace which are beyond speech.

It is life which enables *the richest possible hope*. We cannot live without hope. The will to live here rests upon hope. No surgeon likes to operate on a person who has no desire to live. One recalls Harry Lauder's popular song 'Keep right on to the end of the road'. If that means only this road of time, then is it to be wondered at that hopes should dwindle? For all earthly hopes peter out one by one, the trend for such is always that of diminishing returns until we know what Vernon Bartlett means in his 'retirement' book, *Tuscan Retreat*, when he writes: 'In the final analysis, what is anyone of us doing but killing time until time kills us.' By contrast the Christian knows a life found in time but not bound by it, a life of ever enlarging horizons – eternal life. 'For we know that if the earthly frame that houses us today should be demolished, we possess a building which God has provided – a house not made by human hands, eternal and in heaven' (2 Corinthians 5.1, N.E.B.). So a Christian sings in blessed assurance:

> *In hope that sends a shining ray*
> *Far down the future's broadening way.*

Note that word 'broadening'. The Christian is not as those without hope in God, who in declining years feel it 'narrowing'. 'I am the Resurrection *and the Life*.' He is our 'lively hope', and it is always true that in the life of a true Christian the best is yet to be.

It is a message for the middle years when responsibilities have increased and perhaps disillusionment has

49

been experienced, and there are times when it is realized that 'the waters of the earth have failed and I am thirsty still'. Even the higher delights of home, children, friends, nature, art and literature fail to satisfy the deepest longings, for God has made all desire to remain unsatisfied save in Him. The peril of the middle years is to settle down to life's second best. 'When I was young I thought I might have—', is the beginning of a confession I have often heard from middle-aged lips. How many in the middle years are found experiencing a wistful longing, not dissimilar to the poet's admission: 'And now 'tis little joy to know I'm farther off from heaven than when I was a boy.' Not infrequently I have found that those in the middle years who have missed the gift of life in Christ have what is to them an unexplained disquietude which if they do not seek to forget or stifle it, but are faithful to it, can be God's ministry in the end of enrichment through the gift of new life. 'Quench not the Holy Spirit', for He it is who seeks ever to bring us to that light which is the life of men, whatever our age or circumstance.

It is the message for the aged, for those who are now going down the other side of the hill of life and approaching the valley all men must tread, for all are mortal. Is there a greater tragedy than to approach the valley of death 'without a hope to cheer the tomb', except perhaps to feel no desire or need for one. Personally I find it most difficult to understand one who says 'I am not interested in the question of immortality'. How can anyone mean this who has really loved someone, wife, husband, child, friend, more than oneself, who has now departed this life? There is a Light which transforms the valley of the darkness into 'the valley of the shadow' – shadow is always the result of light. It is never too late in this life to accept Him 'who has brought life and immortality to light through the Gospel', as the dying thief on a cross next to the Cross found, as in his last moments he prayed 'Lord, remember me when Thou comest into Thy kingdom'. The answer, swift and all embracing, was immediate: 'Today shalt thou be with me in Paradise.'

I have always believed and preached, not the superficial advice, 'It's never too late to mend', but the glorious truth that a man can be born again when he is old and so enter and see the kingdom of heaven, as Jesus himself declared to Nicodemus (who, I suspect from his question, was getting on in years). Yet I recall an experience in my personal interviews which I can never forget, which made the lesson of the story Jesus told of the foolish virgins more real to me, and especially the words 'and the door was shut' and they thus discovered it was too late. A man (well on in years) came to my little study one night, who, after a time, described his life of sin, muddle and waste. I saw no reason to doubt the veracity of his confession, which was a story of such degradation that I knew later what Henry Drummond once said he felt he needed after similar confession, a bath as well as prayer. Relying on the guidance and power of the Holy Spirit, in due course I offered him a new life, a cleansed and forgiven heart, and pleaded with all earnestness for trust in Christ. If ever I felt I wrestled with the Devil in man it was that night, and though we were engaged in quiet conversation, when I said goodnight to him some hours later, I discovered I was soaking in perspiration and utterly fatigued. He came the following two Saturday nights. I have learned and I am still learning all I can from such masters of Christian psychology as

Dr Leslie Weatherhead, and others, and I was satisfied this man was not a purely psychological case but a sinner whom grace alone could save. At times his eyes showed a slight gleam of hope, but even as they did it was as though the Devil extinguished it, and always his reply was, 'It is too late'. When saying goodnight for the third Saturday, I assured him that night or day I was available to him. He thanked me most courteously, wished he had met me sooner, said: 'I wish I could believe what you say, but it is too late.' Not long afterwards I read in the evening paper that he had taken his own life. Yet I still believe with all my soul that 'There is life for a look at the Crucified One. There is life at this moment for you.' To quote these words brings me to the very heart of the message of the personal evangelist – the Cross of Christ.

For it is life from death – the death of Him who died to make me good. I noticed in a booklet containing questions for group discussion the question 'What was the most important thing Jesus ever did?' My answer would be 'to *choose* to die as He did for us men and for our salvation'.

> *Didst Thou not die that I might live*
> *No longer to myself but thee,*
> *Might body, soul and spirit give*
> *To Him who gave Himself for me?*
> *Come then, my Master and my God,*
> *Take the dear purchase of Thy blood.*

CHARLES WESLEY (M.H.B. 558)

The Cross is the unchanging revelation of God's mercy and judgement. We cannot know mercy without judgement, and Jesus confirmed God's judgement of sin and at the same time identified himself with man, the sinner, offering His sinless life for us men and our salvation. In it all God was in Christ making possible this blessed reconciliation between our sin-estranged lives and His holy, loving, eternal fellowship. 'Christ was innocent of sin, and yet for our sake God made him one with the sinfulness of men, so that in him we might be made one with the goodness of God himself' (2 Cor. 5.21, N.E.B.). All sin, every sin, leads to the Cross. In Psalm 51, traditionally David's lament and repentance, he never mentions the woman with whom he committed adultery and her husband whose death he devised. He knew he had sinned against God's holy love. 'Against Thee, Thee only have I sinned and done this evil in Thy sight.' We not only grieve but pierce His heart of love by our sin. The Cross is not only the final exposure and condemnation of our sin – yours and mine – but the eternal revelation of His forgiving and redeeming love. There is an awful finality about Calvary – it is God's last word to man, and man's last hope. God has come to us in Christ that we might come to Him and He can do no more than has been done for our salvation.

The Bible is quite explicit about the personal motives and moods which led to the Crucifixion. 'For envy they delivered him up.' Many of the chief rulers believed on him but for fear they would not confess him. 'For they loved the praise of men more than the praise of God.' Indifference, unholy compromise, envy, fear, pride, self concern, jealousy, all these motives and attitudes lead to the Cross of 'shame and scoffing rude'. We need not ask the question of the Negro spiritual: 'Were you there when they crucified my Lord?' We know the answer must be expressed in spiritual terms.

Men still commit the sins which crucify Him afresh, prayerlessness, worldliness, unbelief and indifference to God's call and claims. We are guilty of the greatest of sins, the sin of not believing in Him with such commitment as to be willing to die for Him. For if, as is true, He died to make us good, then we must die to self and sin to become alive in Him. The message then is life through death, and all real life begins at the Cross.

We come to realize also that it is not the best that *I* can be but the best that He can make me which is my truest need and deepest desire. Our failure in the light of his Presence and the knowledge that as Dr Russell Maltby once said, 'we have all spoilt our lives', leads us to realize our utter dependence on Him and our need for repentance and trust in Him. Awareness of sin is the result of awareness of God. Hence the truth expressed in the words of 'They who fain would serve Thee best are conscious most of wrong within'. John Wesley preached law then grace. The law as given in the commandments and the Beatitudes and the Gospel of Grace whereby we are enabled to fulfil by love the law of God. We should challenge the conscience, and especially in these days regarding the sin of 'accidie' (one of the Seven Deadly Sins) or, as I would put it, the 'couldn't care less' answer to Him who couldn't care more. This was one of the sins that brought Christ to the Cross, namely in action, indifference and disregard of the urgency of the Gospel. Present Christ as the supreme life and example of how to live and let the Holy Spirit convict of sin, 'Of sin because they believe not on me', said Jesus.

Two hymns begin with the same opening words. One is 'Just as I am young, strong and free, To be the best that I can be For truth and righteousness and thee, Lord of my life, I come.' If we begin there and are quite serious in asking Christ to take up his abode in our heart and seek in earnest to live in obedience to Him, we shall soon come to know that we are not free and not strong enough to follow His blessed example. Not until utter dependence upon Him, in trust in His atoning sacrifice, in humble gratitude for His gift of enabling love and power shall we know the meaning of His salvation and liberating grace. Then we shall sing: 'Just as I am without one plea but that Thy blood was shed for me and that Thou bidd'st me come to Thee, O Lamb of God, I come.'

No one can fully explain the mystery of the Cross, but all can experience the peace and liberation and reconciliation with God accomplished for us there. 'Repentance toward God and trust in our Lord Jesus Christ' was and is the historic, unchanged Gospel to be interpreted as the Holy Spirit inspires in words and acts understandable by every generation. The continuity of the experience remains the same, hence John the seer, in the first Christian century is one with Charles Wesley in the eighteenth. John wrote in his doxology of praise for Christ's redeeming work as having 'loosed us from our sins' (Revelation 1.5). Wesley expressed the same experience in his well-known hymn 'And can it be . . .' (M.H.B. 371), and in particular in this verse:

> *Long my imprisoned spirit lay*
> *Fast bound in sin and nature's night;*
> *Thine eye diffused a quickening ray—*
> *I woke, the dungeon flamed with light;*
> *My chains fell off, my heart was free,*
> *I rose, went forth and followed Thee.*

Jesus who was 'born of a woman, born under the law' affirmed by His death the righteousness of God's law of the penalty of sin which is death, and for one brief period on the Cross experienced 'the death of deaths' – which is spiritual death, that is the exclusion from the knowledge of God's presence – such is my understanding of the cry of desolation: 'My God, My God, why hast thou forsaken me?' That these words are of a Psalm which Jesus heard and learned as a boy was not an indication of delirium but the truest expression, so I believe, of what He momentarily experienced. Jesus does not promise escape from physical death but from that death to be feared above all else – loss of God's presence.

I know of no clearer description of the experience of the Gospel of Christ Crucified than that of John Wesley, expressed on May 24th, 1738. It was not until he was thirty-five years of age that he became a 'Twice Born' Christian. 'I felt my heart strangely warmed. I felt I did trust in Christ, Christ alone for salvation, and an assurance was given unto me that He had forgiven my sins, even mine, and freed me from the law of sin and death.' He realized for the first time that he himself could do nothing about his need so trusted Christ to deal with it, and thus knew that Christ was not only the Saviour of the world but John Wesley's Saviour. He was freed *from* that he might be freed *to* – to become under God the founder of the Methodist Church with its community of 50 millions at work in 86 countries in the world today – to be indeed the best John Wesley that God could make him. This is the message of life – here and hereafter – for you and me, and for every man.

Recall John Wesley's answers to Mr Spangenberg when he arrived at Savannah, as recorded in his

Journal for February 8th, 1736. 'Do you know Jesus Christ?' I paused and said, 'I know He is the Saviour of the world.' 'True', replied he, 'but do you know He has saved you?' I answered, 'I hope He has died to save me'. He only added, 'Do you know yourself?' I said, 'I do.' But I fear they were vain words.

CHAPTER FOUR

MYSTERY

'We speak the wisdom of God in a mystery'
(1 Corinthians 2.7).

'To make known the mystery of the Gospel'
(Ephesians 6.19).

'The mystery of Christ' (Colossians 4.3).

IN ONE of the best-known Wesley hymns and, amongst
Methodists, one of the most popular, M.H.B. 371, the
second verse begins: ' 'Tis mystery all' – the better-
known words of that hymn are ' 'Tis mercy all'! Yet it
is out of the sense of mystery that the feeling of adoring
wonder is born as we reflect on God's redeeming love
revealed in Christ on Calvary. The great mystery,
according to Wesley, in this hymn is 'The Immortal
dies'. Christians believe that 'God was in Christ reconciling the world to himself' and Christ certainly died.
'In Him (Christ) dwelt all the fullness of God.' Now,
I am no professional theologian but to me part of the
mystery is revealed in what the pre-existent, cosmic
Christ, the One present with the Father in creation,
accepted as limitations in coming to this world for us
men and our salvation. As usual, Wesley puts it in a
sentence or two:

> *He laid His glory by,*
> *He wrapt Him in our clay.*

'What is God like?' The question is often truly answered in the words: 'He is like Jesus', an answer based on His own claim: 'He that hath seen me hath seen the Father', but that is not to claim that he has seen all the attributes of God. To take but one example, Jesus did not claim omniscience. He did not know everything. He confessed that knowledge of the last day was not in His possession. 'But of that day and that hour knoweth no man, no, not the angels in heaven, *neither the Son*, but the Father' (Mark 13.32, A.V. – author's italics). I may quote one further example. Jesus did not know in advance that at a certain hour He would be wearied, seek rest by the side of a well, send His disciples into a village so that He might be alone, and that a certain woman would come at mid-day to collect water there (a most unusual thing to do at that time of day) with the memorable results described in John 4. To say that He had foreknowledge of each detail would rob, for me, the story of its beauty, truth and indeed reality. Yet that Jesus has Divine power, was indeed the Son of God, could have exercised that power to prevent His arrest in Gethsemane, could have answered the taunt of the thief on the Cross to 'save thyself and us' and that of his murderers: 'He saved others, himself he cannot save' is what many Christians believe. All of which, and so very much more, explains Wesley's words:

> '*Tis mystery all! The Immortal dies:*
> *Who can explore His strange design?*
> *In vain the first-born seraph tries*
> *To sound the depths of love divine.*

Now the relevance of this chapter is in relation to what is called the modern mind. In parenthesis, I personally regret modern thoughtlessness rather than modern thought. Yet the personal evangelist must face the fact that it is harder – that is in my own experience – to make a convert now than twenty years ago or even ten years. The scientific atmosphere which is all-pervading has encouraged a scepticism concerning anything which is not susceptible of scientific analysis. The statement of the sixth-former that he no longer believed in God 'because science has explained God away', whether voiced or not, is the attitude of millions of people in this Christian country to which we belong. It is not without significance that the most recent address I gave to boys in our Newcastle Grammar School dealt, at their request, with belief in God; and that some years ago, when I led for a University debate in opposing the motion that 'This House believes that science is of greater importance to progress than religion' we only carried the day by a narrow majority. That I would humbly suggest was not due to our feeble presentation, for I had an excellent seconder.

Dr William Barclay and Mr Malcolm Muggeridge, in a recent discussion in 'Meeting Point' on BBC 1, differed in the view whether man was more or less aware of God in the twentieth century as compared with the first century. My own recollection and impression is that men are less aware of the existence of God, Heaven and Hell now than when I was a boy. Two world wars, the decline in church attendance, the passing of family prayers, the neglect of Bible reading, the diminishing attendance at Sunday School, the failure of parental example and discipline have all tended more and more to produce a godless age. The intellectual attack on the Christian faith is directed against the element of the supernatural. Yet Christian conversion is the supernatural work of the Holy Spirit and will always be so. Despite the honest attempt of the Bishop of Woolwich in *Honest to God* to try to bridge the gulf, the sophisticated intellectual and sometimes pseudo-scientist rules out the validity of the supernatural. Thomas, of the first twelve disciples, has his modern counterparts who demand 'proof', and consider religious faith irrational though most illogically expressing faith in scores of ways in other matters of life. There are those trusting intellect alone who honestly find it difficult to enter the Kingdom; and the more brilliant the mind, often the more difficult it is to appreciate and still more to accept the condition of humility and trust laid down by Christ as necessary: 'Except ye become as little children, ye shall in no wise enter the Kingdom.' For in the end it is trust in Christ, expressed in taking His words seriously and acting on His promises, that make a Christian.

I have not forgotten that Peter, in his first epistle, enjoins Christians to 'be ready always to give an answer to every man that asketh you a *reason* of the hope that is in you'. It is not given to mortals to comprehend the Infinite Greatness of God, though we may apprehend all necessary truth for this life and beyond in Christ. Yet for the Christian, faith is a reasonable faith. It 'stands to reason' for example, so far as I am concerned, to believe that creation began as the Bible begins: 'In the beginning God'. After all, your only choice is between God and Luck. Evolution as a process (with still some doubtful or missing links) does not disprove God's providential wisdom and power, and it certainly does not account for the beginning of life on this planet. If scientists discover how to 'create' life, will they not use material which has already been created without their aid, including their own mental capacity with its often unexplained insights? The atom was here before it was split. This is not the place to develop the argument further, but it is referred to because of the present-day challenge to belief in the mystery of the supernatural, and the appeal of the humanist philosophy of life which is anti-supernatural.

As I write, I have in mind a man of considerable intellectual capacity and other gifts, with whom I made contact through a television series I gave on the subject 'It's my belief'. Ever since, I have prayed for him daily and continue to do so, and he knows the reason. We have had several talks, but his rejection of the Christian faith is on the grounds of reason. I do not question his sincerity, I am satisfied that he is not happy about his present conclusion, but always his verdict is 'I cannot accept anything to which my reason cannot assent or understand'. I am not unmindful of the commandment: 'Thou shalt love the Lord thy God with all thy mind . . .' Reason is surely one of God's greatest gifts to man, raising him above all the lower creations which God subjected to man's dominance. But what my friend is saying is '*my* reason is the final arbiter'. Now faith is the soul's explorer which goes beyond reason. Every Christian realizes that there are things above reason though not necessarily contrary to it. In the presence of the Almighty and Infinite God, he is humble enough to acknowledge the limitations of a human finite mind. Moreover, he believes in what a recent President of the British Association mentioned in the closing sentence of his Presidential address, namely: 'the natural perversity of man'. The Bible calls this the result of man's sin and disobedience to God. It states that spiritual things are spiritually discerned' and Paul described those unaware of God and unbelievers as spiritually blind. 'In whom the God of this world hath blinded the minds of them that believe not, lest the light of the glorious gospel of Christ who is the image of God should shine unto them' or as an alternative translation has it: 'So as to shut out the radiancy of the Gospel of Christ.' Cromwell's plea that we might acknowledge the possibility of being mistaken has point to those who trust in their reason alone.

I remember how vividly it came home to me without, I can honestly and humbly say, any trace of 'holier than thou' attitude, but with a heartfelt pity and compassion, as I talked to a man at his door one afternoon in house-to-house visitation. He told me he had lost whatever faith he ever had in God or man as the result of his experiences in the war. To judge or condemn him was unthinkable, for would I have been any different were it not for the grace of God? The major impression on my heart in the interview was the utter inability to feel any desire, or realize any need for the good things of the Gospel, either for his own sake or that of his family, his country or the world. I remember it coming almost as a shock, the realization that he was blind, not that he required spectacles, as I do, but that he was spiritually blind. We parted on the most affable terms. He really seemed to appreciate my interest in him, but there seemed to him no point in a further conversation. 'I feel quite all right as I am.' The door was shut, and as I walked away I felt in some measure what our Lord felt when He said of those in His own day: 'Thou knewest not the time of thy visitation.' Yet we should never give up hope. There are no 'impossible' people in Christ's sight. We write off so many people because we say they are not interested, but when we speak to them are we as interesting as we should be in telling of 'a lively hope' and of what we know and believe to be true?

I dealt earlier in this chapter with the present-day intellectual challenge – important but by no means as widespread as might be supposed from books and articles written on the subject – because this book might be criticized on the ground that it by-passes the changed world and thought atmosphere in which the personal evangelist has to work, as compared, for example, with that of my father, whose influence had such a profound and lasting effect upon me. I fully recognize the changes in the world since his day. The problem of communicating the Gospel to the present age is a constant challenge to me, though Jesus encountered this problem in talking of the supernatural to Nicodemus, a *religious* intellectual expert. Certain truths, however, remain the same as when I was a boy, and indeed down the centuries. The heart of God revealed for all time in 'Jesus Christ the same yesterday, today and for ever'; the heart of man, for 'He has put eternity into man's mind', making time with its birthdays, calendar months and years insufficient for man's immortal capacity and potentiality. Augustine's words are relevant to every age, for they are true, 'Thou hast made us for Thyself and our hearts are restless until they rest in Thee'. Cecil Rhodes' oft-repeated complaint, 'Too little time, so much to do', is every man's experience who has a zest for life. The utter, amazing relevance of the Gospel for every need of man, here and hereafter is the same. Finally, so is the phrase of Thomas Binney's great hymn, 'A Holy Spirit's energies', for in these is our hope of receiving an enlightened mind, spiritual vision, a transforming revelation from God and of God which enables the opening of the blind eyes, the releasing of the soul from the prison of the bondage of self and sin by Christ the Deliverer.

I shall never forget seeking through a prolonged interview to make the way of salvation clear to one in need of the Saviour, who was 'not far from the Kingdom'. Several times, as I proceeded, he said: 'Yes, I see', but I could not rid myself of the feeling that he did not see. Then in a completely changed tone of voice I realized that the Spirit had been doing His own wonderful work as he had talked, for he suddenly said: 'Yes, I see *now*', and I knew that he did, and an almost became an altogether Christian as we subsequently knelt in prayer and he gave himself to Christ.

Yes, it is a mystery – 'how can a man be born when he is old?' – but it is the wisdom of God, and a mystery which is the blessed reality attested by a multitude now past numbering. Christians through Christ, who is 'the wisdom and power of God' know that reality – 'having made known unto us the mystery' – and therefore are able to make it known to others. They are released by God's revelation, not reason alone, and are able to release others from the tyranny of the devil and from the bondage of time, sin and death.

This is the experience which accounts for the great affirmations of the Christian faith. The testimony of the New Testament is not 'it may be so', or 'perhaps some day it might be possible', or 'I'm not sure and I don't think anybody can be'. Affirmation, not agnosticism, is the dominant note. 'We know', 'you know', 'I know' is the repeated assurance. So the paradox – and the Christian faith abounds with paradox – ('that which is apparently absurd, but really true' – Oxford Dictionary) is that from personal experience of the revealed secret of the Divine Mystery comes the assurance, not that 'All's right with the world', but that all is made right between me and God. A Christian is never sure of himself, but is sure of God and therefore of everything that matters, that it is God's world and that His love and its purposes will triumph in all things in the end.

Part of the work of a personal evangelist is to help one who seeks to become a Christian to receive this blessed assurance, which is one of many reasons for knowing the Bible well with its many promises of assurance. Begin with this one: 'The Spirit himself (not 'itself' as in A.V.) beareth witness with our spirit that we are children of God' (Romans 8.16). 'The witness of the Spirit' once denounced as presumption is the truth in Dr Russell Maltby's mind when he writes these memorable words. 'This, that God deals with us as 'persons' – that when He forgives us one by one, and tells us one by one, that when God receives a sinner unto His family He finds means to let him know'. This then is not self assurance – that is never enough, and is bound sooner or later to fail you. I noticed in an advertisement enclosed in a *Readers' Digest* magazine, 'At 65 . . . self assurance is not enough' and it went on to commend insurance, and on the back of the card I read: 'As you grow older, your concern for the future may change to anxiety.' It often does, but to be assured of Christ in us is to know the perfect love which casteth out all fear. We need not fear anything which may come to us, for we know *who* will come. The word assurance means not only safety or security, but the ability to tell positively that you possess a humble, holy confidence. Luke declares, in his opening word of his

Gospel, his intention to write of 'those things most surely believed among us' and his purpose 'that you may know the truth' (R.S.V.), 'the solid truth' (Moffatt), 'reliable information' (Phillips), 'know the certainty' (Revised), and 'so as to give you authentic knowledge' (N.E.B.). There are many things that Christians then and now do not know, but certain things they do know and can be sure they know. It should be stressed that it is personal assurance: 'Blessed assurance, Jesus is mine.' John Bunyan said: 'It was with joy that I told my wife, O now I know, I know'. In his *History of England* G. M. Trevelyan (one time Regius Professor of Modern History in the University of Cambridge and later Chancellor of my own University of Durham) writes of John Wesley declaring 'a personal assurance of salvation bringing new birth and dominion over sin'. In the biography of John Henry Newman, *The Pillar of the Cloud*, Meriol Trevor, referring to Newman's conversion, states: 'This mysterious event to him for ever more certain than that he had hands or feet. . . .'

It is the current fashion to deplore dogma and certainty. It is so easy through being dogmatic to become intolerant. An open mind, so open sometimes that it retains nothing more definite than its openness is the present vogue. Opinions are preferred to convictions, and the advocate of this frame of mind points to the changes in medicine, education and science which, in a decade or less, demand the revision of text books and the substitution of new ideas. A Christian believes there is new truth to break forth from God's Word, or rather new aspects and appreciations of truth hitherto denied us because of our inability to receive them. 'I have yet many things to say unto you but you cannot bear them now', said Jesus to his first disciples. Truth waits upon truth, as every teacher knows. First the alphabet, then the spelling of simple words, until we come to the stage when we can read and enjoy great literature.

My own personal beliefs form into three circles. Firstly, there are those which are vital to me, and though not many in number, mean everything to me and of which I am blessedly assured. These form the inner circle. The second circle consists of beliefs which are important, but not crucial. Beyond that, there is an outer circle in which I am a Christian agnostic, meaning: 'It may be so but I cannot say for certain.' The secret of the mystery becomes an increasing knowledge, and assurance through obedience to His will. Jesus declared this was the way to know – to obey.

In what, then, is our assurance centred? The answer is in Christ and His unfailing promises. 'He whose word cannot be broken.' His finished work for us brings its own assurance as He works in us and through us.

We may be assured in the first instance of that primary and essential blessing offered to us in Christ, namely forgiveness of our sin. The explanation of God's redeeming love we can never fully understand, but we can experience it.

> *Love moved Him to die,*
> *And on this we rely;*
> *He hath loved, He hath loved us:*
> *   we cannot tell why;*
> *But this we can tell,*
> *He has loved us so well*
> *As to lay down His life to redeem*
> *   us from hell.*

CHARLES WESLEY

We may be assured that both our life, and whatever we do in His name and for His sake, are in His secure and eternal keeping 'I know whom I have believed and am assured He is able to keep that which I have committed unto Him against that day' is Paul's assurance that can be ours – which I believe meant both his work and his life. He wrote this when in prison, but he knew, as F. D. Maurice pointed out, that 'God can take care of his own cause'. We may be assured of the life to come, not detailed knowledge but all that it is necessary to know to sustain 'the hope that is in you'. 'We know that if our earthly house of this tabernacle were dissolved, we have a building of God, a house not made with hands, eternal, in the heavens' (2 Corinthians 5.1). 'As we have born the earthly so, shall we bear the heavenly image.' 'If it were not, so' said Jesus, 'I would have told you. I go to prepare a place for you. . . . I will come again and receive you unto myself.' In the meantime we know that 'All things work together for good to them that love God', to the end that we may be made ready for His call to the higher service. We know by this what is His over-riding will in all things, namely goodness and our good. 'For this is the will of God, even your sanctification'. ' 'Tis mystery all', ' 'Tis mercy all', and all is in that wonderful assurance with which Wesley ends his hymn: 'through Christ my own.'

The Rev. Tom Dring, in one of his prayers with me, said: 'We thank you, Heavenly Father, for our inner certainties.' In this age of so much uncertainty and change, when men's hearts fail them from fear and so many young people are uncertain and confused, what an opportunity is presented to the personal evangelist who is possessed of inner certainties.

As personal evangelists, we need to seek continually, by prayer, study and experiment, to find the best ways of presenting the truth of the Gospel to our own age. We are to be in the world but not of it (John 17.14, 15, 16) and the essential Gospel is the same: for whilst the circumstances of life change the basic needs of the human heart remain the same. We need continually to examine and re-examine the structure of the Church that it may be the instrument God desires and can use in the world of today for the spread of the Gospel. We need the fellowship of the Church for the nurture and growth of new-born souls. We need the daily help of the Holy Spirit to edify and build us up in our most holy faith. And always we need more and more personal evangelists who will challenge the indifferent, arouse the careless and apathetic, stimulate the curiosity that can lead to consecration and bring men and women, old and young, one by one to the Saviour who died to make us good and who lives as the only hope of the world. Personal evangelism is indispensable to the furtherance of the Gospel, and that means personal evangelists in every church. *It means you and me.*

It begins in friendship, but its purpose is the saving friendship of Christ. I remember reading of a gifted leader and lover of the Christian Church Clubs movement declaring that his greatest worry was that in many cases we are no different from the secular youth organizations of our day and then, in heavy type the words 'Our evangelism is lost in our friendship.' A recent letter in the *Methodist Recorder*, written by that fine youth leader the Rev. Reg Bedford, dealt with the opportunities of youth service in various parts of the world but added some wise cautionary words which included the following: 'It is important that the drive for service projects should be linked with an understanding of the Christian reasons for such action. Otherwise even voluntary service can be an escape from the real challenge of commitment to Christ.' Personal evangelists worthy of the name are involved in the need, suffering and distresses of the world. They seek to dedicate time, talents and money to service of others, Christian or non-Christian, but they ever remember that they are called to share the secret of the mystery revealed to them of God's greatest gift to His children. Their evangelistic concern inspires outreach for men and women as they seek in everything, social justice, radical equality, to bridge the gulf between the haves and the have-nots, thus expressing the mind of Christ and serving Him by serving the least of these His brethren.

All Christians then can engage in some work of personal evangelism through prayer, witness, service and speech to the end that there may be added daily to the Church such as are being saved. The greatest need of Britain is for more Christian homes, which implies Christian parents. The greatest need of the world is for real Christians. Personal evangelists ever seek to add to the number.

Alas! It is possible to talk about evangelism, to have conference after conference and not to do the work personally. 'Do the work of an evangelist', wrote Paul to Timothy. He didn't say, 'Call a conference to consider it or talk about it', he said: '*Do it!*' 'The greatest need today is to get individuals inviting individuals to Christ', says Dr Harry Denman, described as Methodism's Elder Statesman of evangelism in America. 'Many churchgoers – even preachers, missionaries and evangelists bother little at all about the spiritual taste of those with whom they rub shoulders. . . . Many prominent evangelists would have to admit that it has been years since they have on their own initiative sought out a single person with the intention of seeing him find a saving faith in Christ.' I am not able to confirm, myself, the truth of these words which I read in an article by the News Editor of the American edition of *Christianity Today* for March, 1967. But do we not all need to ask the question which each of his disciples put to our Lord so long ago: 'Lord, is it I?' We should each ask ourselves if we are failing him and by our silence denying others the good news. We can and often do, but we need not do so any longer. We can offer ourselves here and now 'to make known the mystery of the Gospel'. We can pray for 'a sense of what is vital' to its proclamation and for the fullness of the Holy Spirit to empower us – *and then act accordingly.*

Sir George Williams, the Founder of the Y.M.C.A. was asked by his close friend, Dr. John R. Mott: 'What was primarily in your mind and in the minds of those associated with you when you formed the first group which later became known as the Young Men's Christian Association?' 'We had only one idea', he said, 'which was that we might be made helpful in leading the young fellows round about us to Jesus Christ.' In a final interview with this wonderful Christian evangelist, when his physical weakness in old age made difficult sustained thought and conversation, he nevertheless had moments of bright and wonderously clear vision. During one of these he said to the same friend: 'You are never with a man, are you? but you talk to him about Jesus Christ.' This word of Sir George Williams shows his undying passion for the winning of men for Christ, and it should be ours, too.

CHAPTER FIVE

THE MOTIVE

'The very spring of our actions is the love of Christ'
                                        (2 Corinthians 5.14).

CHRIST's love for us and our consequent love for Him is the supreme motive from which issues our love for our fellow men who are all God's children. The essence of love is sharing in the fullest and most intimate way with the beloved one so that every day throughout life we become more one in thought, desire, purpose and partnership. Surely this is what lies behind the words: 'O for a closer walk with God.' It might be expected, therefore, that marriage, as the most intimate human relationship, would be used to illustrate this spiritual relationship which is indeed just what the Bible does. 'And I will betroth thee unto me for ever' is God's word in the Old Testament, and in the New Testament the church is described as The Bride of Christ'.

As in everything, God takes the initiative, for always it is true: 'In the beginning God.' Every Christian becomes a Christian through the communion of the Holy Spirit revealing the love of God expressed in the grace of our Lord Jesus Christ. And this transforming experience of truth is personal. 'He loved me and gave Himself for me', said the one-time enemy of the Christian faith, the great Apostle Paul. And the Apostle John, with the insight of great love for Christ, wrote:

'Herein is love, not that we loved God but that He loved us and sent his Son to be the propitiation for our sins', and then he sums it up in eight memorable words: 'We love him because he first loved us.'

As in human marriage with true love there is a growing sense of indebtedness, oft expressed in the words: 'I don't know what I would do without you.' Even so, in our increasing dependence upon Him, we know that 'Life means Christ to me' (Philippians 1.2 1, Moffatt) and sing from our hearts the words: 'O to grace how great a debtor daily I'm constrained to be.' It is this knowledge of the love of Christ, all He did for me by His death, all He does for me by His Living Presence in me, all His rich and utterly trustworthy promises to me which place me in a life-long obligation to make Him known to every other man and woman. 'Woe is me if I preach not the Gospel.' My namesake, John Pawson, one of Wesley's Helpers, who subsequently became President of the Methodist Conference, said: 'Having found salvation myself I felt an intense desire that others should enjoy the same unspeakable blessing.' It is ever the same in a truly converted life, I mean the desire to share 'glad tidings of good things' as Paul described the Gospel. From *New Singer, New Song* by David Winter, I learn that Pop Star Cliff Richard in 1960 wrote: 'Whatever else becomes public one's own beliefs should be private.' In 1967, he stood beside Billy Graham and from London proclaimed to millions: 'I feel it is my duty and the duty of all Christians to tell as many people as possible about the wonderful thing I have discovered. . . . It works, it works for me. Until you have taken the step of asking Christ into your life your life is not really worth while.' John Wesley had four tests of a Christian and number four was: 'Have I found something which I feel a burning desire to pass on to others?'

Listen to Jeremiah: 'If I say I will not make mention of him, nor speak any more in his name, then there is in my heart as it were a burning fire and I weary myself to hold it, but cannot.' Recall the story of the lepers who discovered the hastily abandoned Syrian camp of Israel's enemies with all its resources of food, clothing, silver and gold and their remembrance of the famished Israelites whose city they had left behind in their desperate need. 'We do not do well: this is a day of good tidings and we hold our peace. . . . Now therefore come that we may go and tell' (2 Kings 7.9). Paul implies that we are in debt to our fellow men until we tell them of the Gospel: 'I am under obligation (debtor, A.V.) to Greek and non-Greek, to learned and simple; hence my eagerness to declare the Gospel to you in Rome as well as to others' (Romans 1.15).

Nothing other than this love for Christ and love for all those for whom He died can explain the sacrifice and faithful service, even unto death, of a countless number of His ambassadors all down the centuries for His sake and that of the Gospel. How else can you account in our own time for those who gave their lives to bring the Gospel to the Auca killer tribe (of the Ecuador Jungle) whose splendid mission is described in the book *Through Gates of Splendour?*

'The love of Christ doth me constrain, To seek the wandering souls of men.' The challenging question to ask ourselves is: are we so constrained? Does the ignorance and spiritual blindness concerning the Gospel on the part of so many cause real pain in our hearts? Have we an abiding concern for those of our fellows living and dying without a personal knowledge of the love and power of God in Christ? I feel sure that it depends upon how precious is the faith and experience we possess in Christ, or how real is our personal knowledge of His saving, enriching and fulfilling grace in our own souls. Do we seek to save men and women for their own sake or to save the church (recalling a one-time Methodist slogan: 'Evangelize or perish')?

We are not primarily concerned with making new church members but with leading people to Christ; given the latter, the former will follow. It is important therefore to get our motive right. We evangelize because we love to obey our Lord and desire to know His joy within us in fulfilling His will. I remember a service I was unexpectedly called upon to conduct thirty years ago when on holiday at Seahouses, in Northumberland. My record shows that I preached from the theme: 'How near are you to Christ?' 'Ye are they which have continued with me in my temptations' (Luke 22.28) and other occasions when our Lord referred to His disciples as being 'with me'. This was, of course, long before the days of being 'with it'. Looking at the manuscript now it seems to be full of weaknesses; nevertheless, I challenged myself and my congregation as to how near we were to Christ (1) In His challenge to evil, (2) in prayer that cost Him blood and (3) in His mission of redemptive suffering. It is this last named which I now think is the key to the true motive for the personal evangelist. 'All I care for is to know Christ, to experience the power of His resurrection, and to share his sufferings in growing conformity with his death.' This was the over-mastering ambition of Paul, to know Him by sharing His sufferings, all of which were for the redemption of the world. Entrusted with the honour and glory of Christ's name and Gospel, a personal evangelist feels infinite pity and burning concern when He is not given His rightful place in individual and corporate life.

Hugh Price Hughes was once asked to conduct an evangelistic campaign in a northern town, and in enquiring about the conditions one of his first questions was: 'How many Christians suffer in the town?' I don't think he meant through persecution, as we do not in general suffer insult, ignominy and malice in the country now as did John Wesley in early years of his evangelism in the eighteenth century. Christians in close, intimate relationship should 'suffer with their Lord below' because of His continuing travail for the lost. Paradoxically, they suffer gladly with Him because they love Him and share the cost and the joy of redemptive love. Once again Paul, whose motive for evangelism is so demonstrable of what I am trying to describe, puts it in these words: 'It is now my happiness to suffer for you. This is my way of helping to complete in my poor human flesh the full tale of Christ's affliction still to be endured.' For this giving of oneself in love to others applies to both converted and unconverted people with whom His providence has linked us, for 'love will never come to an end' (1 Corinthians 13.8. N.E.B.). Conversion is only the beginning and a personal evangelist should be available for help to those born again to enable them to 'Grow in grace and in the knowledge of our Lord and Saviour, Jesus Christ' (2 Peter 3.18). 'A never dying soul to save, and fit it for the sky' – and the fitting ministry can be costly in prayer and loving service. The personal follow up is as important as the decision for Christ. We have to help those young in faith to walk though showing them how to depend on Christ rather than upon us as they develop into mature Christians. All is of love, that love for Christ which becomes identity with Him, and flowing out in love for God's children whether Christian or non-Christian. A passion for Christ is revealed in a passion* for souls, and without this union there is no faithful personal evangelism.

Surely our Lord's question in the garden of Gethsemane: 'Could'st thou not watch one hour?' reveals His longing to share the travail of His redeeming love and purpose. And as He is the same yesterday, today and for ever, if Christ be really formed in us – which was Paul's intense prayer for his converts – we shall feel and desire, pray and act in the closest union with His Indwelling Presence. 'As thou hast sent me into the world, even so have I sent them into the world' (John 17.18) was His prayer for His first disciples and for us, even as is His word when He came to them as the Risen Lord and said: 'As my Father hath sent me, even so send I you' (John 20.21).

James Maxton, in his book on Lenin, wrote of the famous Russian revolutionary leader: 'He demanded more sacrifice than most men were ready to give.' It is true of the greatest leader in time and eternity for He demands 'my soul, my life, my all'. Yet every demand of Jesus has its setting in His love, and He never calls us to anything which His love does not empower us to fulfil. Yet who amongst us in reviewing the cost of our discipleship can honestly speak of sacrifice? How much does intercessory prayer 'take out' of us? Could we

* Oxford Dictionary – from a word meaning *to suffer*. A personal evangelist may have sleepless hours some nights as in agonising prayer he suffers vicariously not just for but *with* those in physical or spiritual need, or both.

ever describe it as agonizing prayer on behalf of the unsaved? In the middle of the nineteenth century a young minister visited Dundee. His work was not flourishing though he served diligently. He had read of Robert Murray M'Cheyne, who had died at thirty, yet had moved Scotland by his passionate evangelism. The young minister was shown round St Peter's Church and given much information about M'Cheyne by the old sexton who had known him. The young minister stood in the hallowed pulpit and opened the Bible under the instruction of his guide who then said, recalling the saintly M'Cheyne: 'Now let the tears flow.' Did not William Booth, the founder of the Salvation Army, in reply to an officer who communicated his failure to make an impression on those indifferent to Christ, after trying several different approaches, send a telegram with the words: 'Try tears.'

I have knelt in that pulpit at St Peter's, Dundee, and prayed that the same Spirit might work in and through me as possessed Robert Murray M'Cheyne. We may not weep in public – though Jesus once wept before His disciples over a city – but we can be moved by the Spirit to thoughts and feelings which are secret tears. Principal George Adam Smith, in his biography of the great lay evangelist Professor Henry Drummond of Edinburgh, writes of his amazing power to lift lust-soaked, wrecked students. 'On his arms they were lifted up.' That means love which does not count the cost and shares the burden of the Cross. This is the deepest meaning of the prayer so often sung: 'O Master, let me walk with Thee.' The source of our outreaching love is our love for the Indwelling Christ. With our Master we are always seeking, regardless of cost, the good of others.

The spring, then, of all our action and reaction in life, is the love of Christ, His love for me, my love for Him, through His life in me. The beauty of Jesus if seen in me is His love inspiring my love for others. The meaning of that love in action is given in Paul's description in 1 Corinthians 13, personified if we substitute the name Christ for the word love in that wonderful chapter. We work out the salvation God works in by loving others in and through His wonderful love. Action is the expression of that love. How often Jesus encouraged people to translate blessing received or desired into action. 'Go tell my disciples and Peter', was His loving command through the angels to the women at the tomb to whom was revealed the fact of the Resurrection, and this was surely *His* inspiring message to them. 'Go sell all that thou hast and give to the poor', was His word to the rich, young ruler, which is the first step if you really want what you say is your desire. To the woman at the well, He said: 'Go call thy husband.' 'Go home to thy friends and tell them how great things the Lord hath done for thee and hath had compassion on thee', He said to one out of whom He had cast devils.

Love in action is the essential evidence of our faith in Christ translating our surrender, our consecration, our vows to Him into loving service for others: and in all our efforts in personal evangelism let us ever keep in mind Charles Wesley's words, 'Our end, the glory of the Lord'.

'How shall we show our love to Thee'? is not only a question for Harvest Festival occasions, but for daily prayer. No words I have seen better express the love motive of the Christian than those of Paulus Gerhardt, translated by John Wesley:

My Saviour! How shall I proclaim,
 How pay the mighty debt I owe?
Let all I have, and all I am,
 Ceaseless to all Thy glory show.

Too much to Thee I cannot give;
 Too much I cannot do for Thee;
Let all Thy love, and all Thy grief,
 Graven on my heart for ever be.

This is the love which accounts for Henry Martyn's desire, in obeying His call to go to India: 'Now let me burn out for God', as it is of a countless number of men and women who have given their all in the service of His love. This is the highest love, *agape*, the love that transcends all other expressions of love, the love that never counts the cost of satisfying the need or desire of the one beloved. This is the love only seen to perfection in Him Who loved us and gave Himself for us, yet required of us if we are truly His own. 'By this shall men know that ye are mine, if ye have love one to another.' 'A new commandment I give unto you, that ye love one another; as I have loved you, that ye also love one another.' He alone can give us this love. He alone can sustain and enrich it in our lives. He alone can give us the power to express it. It is the love which, had he possessed it, would have impelled the elder brother to go into the far country and seek for his prodigal brother that he might bring him home to the father. This is the love which never gives up anyone, however hopeless or impossible they appear to be. This is the love that forgives until 490 times, if need be, by which time you cannot conceive you could do other than forgive. This is the love that never gives up and never lets go. This is, in two words, *Christ's Love*. 'Having loved His own, He loved them to the end'. 'I will never disown you'. A Christian is one in whom Christ lives and loves like that in seeking and saving the lost. He does not preach at people but preaches Christ and loves them into the Kindgom.

When I was a boy in the Newcastle Methodist Mission of which my father was the Superintendent Minister, I became friendly with several men and women who were indeed 'trophies of grace' – (e.g., see story of Geordie, p. 126). One of them was a cabby (in the days of horse-drawn cabs) who was known as one of the hardest drinking men on the Newcastle Central Station cab stand. Alas, he encouraged his wife to share in drinking sprees. One Saturday night he had been drinking so heavily that the publican, wanting to get rid of him, promised to treat some men to drinks if they would take the cabman home, not many streets away. When he woke up from his drunken stupor, he found they had not only taken him home, but had taken his watch (in the days of fewer public clocks so indispensable to a cabman) as well as robbing him of several pounds. He vowed it would be the last day of this kind of life and found his way to the People's Hall (the Mission centre) and there, to use the words I remember which often came from my father's lips in those days, 'he was soundly converted'. As I transcribe this account from my father's pencilled notes which lie beside me, I read: 'And though that is over thirty years ago he has lived such a consistent godly life, he has not given five minutes' anxiety, but hours and hours of rejoicing to those responsible for his pastoral care.' Do actions speak louder than words? Not long after his conversion Tot – for Tot was the only name or nickname I ever heard him called – was seen running after a passenger, who had alighted from his cab. On his return, a fellow cabman asked for an explanation. 'Was he trying a fast one on you, Tot ?' 'No,' replied Tot. 'He gave me half a sovereign over and above my fare and I thought he had mistaken it for a sixpence.' Nothing more was said that night but next day, when some of the cabbies were making fun of Tot for becoming a Christian, the enquiring cabman of the day before stepped forward and said: 'You chaps, shut up. The next man that says aught more against Tot and his religion, I'll knock him down. If religion will make Tot Reed give half a quid for sixpence, there's something in it.' I love that story of how Tot let the love of Jesus shine through a sixpence, but to me a far greater story of Tot, revealing the motive of love for Christ as the spring of all our actions, concerns his relationship with his wife following his conversion. He did all possible to win her for Christ and save her from the sins which were damning her life and for which he held himself partly responsible, but faithful prayer and loving persuasion and all else apparently failed. She made the home a hell, and when Tot returned from services at the Mission it was to find her often with others in a drunken orgy, pouring out from foul lips obscene taunts, hate and blasphemous scorn concerning Tot and his religion. So it continued until it seemed impossible to carry on, as the sight of Tot when she was 'in drink', as they used to say, seemed to inflame the devil in her. Three times a well-known Christian solicitor of the city, a member of the Mission, prepared papers for Tot to sign to enable a legal separation, and each time, when it came to the point of signing, he turned back and said: 'No, I cannot leave her. I

83

encouraged her in our sinful days and I must stand by until the end.' He never knew the particular translation of Paul's confession at the head of this chapter – it wasn't written then – but to me dear, faithful Tot, one of Christ's gentlemen, is the finest interpretation of the passage quoted. I always understood that the life she lived precipitated her death, but when it came Tot was watching over her in love, for, like his blessed Lord, having loved his own he loved to the end.

'If you love only those who love you, what reward can you expect? Surely the tax gatherers do as much as that. And if you greet only your brothers what is there extraordinary about that. You must therefore be all goodness, just as your heavenly Father is all good.' That is another example of the impossibly high standard Jesus sets to unaided man, but with God all things are possible. 'Love your enemies and pray for your persecutors.' Is it inconceivable that Tot Reed could have continued loving as he did without the love of God in his heart?

So often, when quoting the personal words of John Wesley describing his evangelical conversion on the night of May 24th, 1738, I have heard speakers stop short at the end of his testimony about his experience of sins forgiven. Is it not of tremendous significance that he immediately went on to say: 'I began to pray with all my might for those who had in a more especial manner despitefully used me and persecuted me,' – words which I recall, when I first *really* read them, conveyed a surprisingly personal challenge to me, as does the story of Tot and his wife. We might have *begun* our prayer, if in John Wesley's shoes that night, with prayers of thanksgiving for Peter Bohler, the meeting to which he had come 'very unwillingly', the reading of Luther's preface to the Romans and Paul the author of the epistle and other happenings of that day before 'a quarter to nine o'clock' in the evening. No, it was for those whom so many of us Christians cross off (if we ever included them) our prayer list – as perhaps John Wesley had done before that never to be forgotten experience. 'She always gets my back up.' 'He rubs me up the wrong way.' 'I avoid him for my own soul's good.' 'I might forgive, but I could never forget.' 'I'm finished with him and he needn't look to me for any more help.' And these are expressions I have heard from the lips of professing Christians.

'Looking upon the multitudes he had compassion upon them', and they were people of the same stuff of life as we mingle with day by day, just as fickle and foolish, as disappointing and disloyal, as trying and faithless, as selfish and self-seeking as we all are at times until, having seen the highest, we needs must love it. 'For the love of Christ leaves us no choice. . . . His purpose in dying for all was that men while still in life should cease to live for themselves and should live for him.' To fail that love is to fail others, to embrace it is to enfold others in its transforming grace. Should we grieve His Spirit we know we are ashamed and despise ourselves, but when we respond to His love and love others in His Name and for His sake, we know we make glad His heart.

My Professor of Agriculture in earlier student days once gave me a second-hand book which he thought might interest me, entitled *Paul's Joy in Christ*. I have often thought I should like to attempt a companion volume entitled 'Christ's Joy in Paul'. It may have been suggested by words in a letter the well-known Studdert Kennedy penned to his wife from the Front in the first World War. He had met another chaplain out there who greatly impressed him, hence his description ending: 'And God must enjoy him tremendously.' Yes, here again joy, like sunshine, breaks through. For if 'we preach not ourselves but Christ Jesus the Lord and ourselves your servants for Jesus' sake' (2 Corinthians 4.5); if our bodies are a holy, living sacrifice and our lips and lives the channel of His love; if in short the motive is love, then shall we know that of the three gifts by which men live, faith, hope and love, the greatest of these is love. 'Love holds good – everywhere, for everybody, for ever' (*Jesus – Leader and Lord*, Alan T. Dale). To love God and love our fellow men in Christ is to fulfill our destiny. 'Beloved, if God so loved us, we ought also to love one another.' 'Herein is our love made perfect . . . because as He is so are we in this world' (1 John 4.11, 17).

CHAPTER SIX

THE METHODS

'I have, in short, been all things to all sorts of men that by every possible means I might win some to God'
(1 Corinthians 9.22, Phillips's trans.).

THE TITLE of the world-famed book by Helen Keller, namely *The World in Which I Live*, suggested this line of thought which has long afforded me a background to personal methods in evangelism. It is true that we all live in the same world, and it is equally true that we live in different worlds. William James, the Harvard philosopher, once told of a workman about his house with whom he engaged in conversation, who in the course of their chat together observed: 'There's not much difference between one man and another but what there is, is very important.' Dr Inge, one-time Dean of St Paul's, London, was once talking to the then Bishop of London about an anti-Christian movement of thought. The Dean's comment was concise but revealing: 'That hits me where I live', he said, by which he meant, of course not his postal address but the world in which he lived.

Here then are three principles I have sought to apply which consciously, or more often unconsciously, influence my methods in seeking to win men and women for Christ.

I. *The world in which we really live is the world inside not outside.* It was James Russell Lowell who wrote: 'After all the kind of world one carries about within one's self is the important thing and the world outside takes all its grace, colour and value from that.' What we see and find in the outside world depends upon what we are within. 'All things work together for good to them that love God' and 'All these things are against me' are two verdicts upon life found in the Bible, by two men whose lives, though separated by time, contained the same 'stuff of life' in the form of adversity and difficulty. 'In the isle called Patmos' was the geographical description of the concentration camp in which the writer of the final book of the Bible was detained. 'In the Spirit on the Lord's Day' was his description of where he really dwelt. 'O for the wings of a dove, then would I fly away and be at rest' is a popular anthem and gramophone record. Well, we can do it by B.E.A. or B.O.A.C. and fly 'to the uttermost parts' and when we get there the inner world is the same as when we embarked.

If, then, there is chaos, confusion, fear, bitterness, conflict and wars in the world outside – as revealed by the news day by day, is it to be wondered at when we know what obtains in the hearts of men? The outer world reflects the inner one, the unsolved problems of self and sin, the inner conflict and disorder between what we know we ought to be and do and what we really are issue in wars, selfishness, stupid and sinful barriers between man and man. How great then is the need for this prayer:

> *And let our ordered lives confess*
> *The beauty of Thy peace.*

'Keep thy heart with all diligence for out of it are the issues of life.' The world inside is the world in which we really live, and it is hypocritical to seek to make the world outside better if we carry about with us a world inside which needs to be radically changed.

II. *To help anyone, you must seek to understand the world in which he or she really lives*. That takes time, patience, the art of listening and the sight which Jesus always had which was insight. It means what Paul meant in the words quoted at the head of this chapter; not being a 'Yes' man, for he was far from that, but laying yourself in prayerful thought and understanding alongside the other person. It is the God-given gift of inspiring and cultivating the friendship which encourages confidence and sharing of needs and problems and desires which is so important a part of personal pre-evangelism. It is through the exercise of the Spirit's greatest gift, 'holy, heavenly love' – that Christian love for another person which is the expression of utmost, undiscourageable and undefeatable goodwill and longing for the best for another life – which reaches the real inner life of another person *and understands*.

Paul's description of his method of personal evangelism was surely that of seeing things from another person's standpoint. He was certainly not all things to all men in a spirit of unqualified tolerance unquestioning compromise and 'with it' without limits. In thought, desire and dedication to this service for others, he exemplified the spirit of the prophet Ezekiel, whose original intended message to God's people was changed because 'I went and sat down where they sat'. In my early enthusiasm for the cause of Christ, I was not averse to criticism which afforded me an opportunity to demonstrate the superiority of the Christian side. I am afraid I must have sometimes lost my man in winning my case, as Lord Soper declared possible, and in shame I confess it may not always have been done to the glory of God, for it is so easy to desire to justify oneself. I am so thankful that I learned by the grace of God a 'more excellent way'. Whenever in conversation someone makes a blatant, perhaps ignorant and untruthful criticism of the Christian Way of Life, I pause before replying and pray for grace to enable me to discover what lies behind the remark, and what is the background and experience which provoked it. This is the way to helpful understanding. I do not believe that 'to know all is to forgive all' but really, to begin with people where they are, we must seek to see *from the inside* the world in which they live. How much did the elder brother know of the prodigal, even though for years they had lived and worked together on the same farm? For that matter, how much do we really know about those we live and work with day by day or worship with on Sunday in the same church year after year? How much do we try to know and understand? On holiday, when I have time to scan several newspapers, it is interesting and not without educational value to see the varying interpretations given to the same facts of that outside world of daily happenings. Much is said and written in these days about Christians becoming involved in the secular world and so often the subject is treated in abstract and ambiguous terms. Involvement in another life in the work of personal evangelism is costly in its demand for a caring, sharing and continuing concern in personal relationship. From Christ we prayerfully learn the humble, loving (above all else) understanding approach, desiring to be of service in the particular situation and to enable God to enter into it. This was how the Master acted and the Gospel records abound in illustrations. Paul began with people where they were – See Acts 17. 23 (N.E.B.) 'For as I was going round looking at the objects of your worship I noticed among other things an altar bearing the inscription "To an Unknown God". What you worship but do not know – this is what I now proclaim.' For many this approach is relevant today for judging by various polls and surveys made in recent years a large proportion of the public believes in the existence of God – but do not know Him. It also shows an attempt to grapple with the philosophic difficulties of thoughtful people, which is an important part of evangelism today. The personal evangelist will read and study as time permits anything which will assist him to know better the mood, culture and trends of our changed and changing world. Only thus can he learn to be more effective and, as Charles Wesley writes, 'serve the present age, my calling to fulfil'.

III. *It is both the privilege and responsibility of a Christian to reveal to others the difference Christ makes to the world within.* This is personal witness which, like all other gifts of God, can be used to His glory or so marred by the devil as to glorify self. 'The function of the Church in this world is to make life in this world a poor thing by comparison', said Dr John Hutton. In what I consider one of the best publications of our Church, namely *The Message and Mission of Methodism*, there occurs in the conclusion this sentence, which has long been a challenge to me: 'Sooner or later every church must ask itself the question "What have we to offer?" ' I substitute Christian for the word Church and then, being a member of the church, ask of myself: 'What have *I* to offer?' It is, of course, true that our whole life should be an unconscious declaration which provides both the comparison and offer stated in these quotations. It is equally true that there must be a conscious application of the same witness. It is a subtle temptation of the devil which leads Christian people to rely chiefly, if not almost entirely, on what is oft described as the silent, unconscious witness of the life. If our life is not a commentary on what we say with our lips, then our words may be turned into an argument against, rather than for, the Christian cause. Nevertheless reticence can be as harmful as unguided speech, and it is not always what Christians say, but what they don't say, which hinders and misrepresents the work of God. Our reticence can arise from a false humility or a self-conscious fear of being misunderstood. Aren't we all more or less inhibited from the fear of 'parading our belief'? Silence can be disloyalty and ingratitude.

Here there is the indispensable need of the Holy Spirit in all expression of personal evangelism. We must seek daily by continuing prayer, and prayer which is translated into life and action to seek to obey His leading and prompting in declaring our personal experience. We must never cease to pray for the right word to the right person at the right time – when all three synchronize then we can believe and know that 'no word from Thee can fruitless fall'. We must pray to be delivered from mistaking impulse for God's inner voice, and zeal for expression from zeal for God. Without His guidance and utter dependence upon Him for the promised word in the time of need – 'in that hour it shall be given you' – we shall blunder and may do more harm than good. Yet can anyone be true to his calling in Christ who is either a secret or silent Christian? If we are to preach (to offer Christ) then we must mean the words we often sing, and perhaps too easily, 'Take my lips and let them be filled with messages from Thee.' 'Lord, speak to me, that I may speak.' There must no qualification regarding time, place, or circumstances on our part in these prayers expressed in our hymns, they should mean consciously that we desire to be used *in this way*: 'Just as Thou wilt and when and where.' To confine preaching to pulpits, churches and Sundays is the tragic mistake on the part of so many Christians.

There are several different words in the Greek New Testament which are nearly always translated into our English Bible by the single word 'preach' or 'preaching'. Mark 2.2, I think, would be more accurately translated 'Jesus talked to them about God and His ways' – in short a conversation. Another word used when Paul preached so long that a young man fell asleep, and fell from the window-sill where he was sitting, is one from which we get dialogue or discussion. Possibly Paul went on after his address answering and discussing questions. In Acts 8.25 (N.E.B.) it says 'after giving their testimony and speaking the word of the Lord they took the road back to Jerusalem, bringing the good news to many Samaritan villages on the way'. Here it has been suggested the word used could be translated 'gossip' even as John Bunyan described three or four women of Bedford talking about the things of God as they sat in the sun. ('Methought they spake as though joy did make them speak'.) It was a setback to the progress of preaching the Gospel when Christians began to confine preaching the word to pulpits, churches, ministers and Sundays. How much we need the natural conversational testimony to the worthwhileness of the Christian faith in all the common ways and activities of life.

Opportunities for witness abound, e.g., when thanked for a service rendered, when seeking to comfort the suffering or bereaved or helping those enslaved with worry or anxiety, when asked for guidance or discussing personal, national, or world problems, when congratulating others or being congratulated by them on recovery from illness (with due mention of those God has used to mediate His healing power) – in short in living and working with others. 'In all thy ways acknowledge Him. . . .' (Proverbs 3.6). We sing 'O for a thousand tongues', but how much we need to pray 'Unloose our stammering tongues to tell, Thy love, immense, unsearchable'. Remember the promise and experience of Pentecost which is for *every* Christian. Spirit-filled lives are empowered to speak.Apostolic preaching was everywhere. 'But they went out to make their proclamation everywhere' (Mark 16.20, N.E.B.).

This witness to the world within, fashioned and furnished by Christ, is one of the incentives to the increasing possession of what Wesley described as scriptural holiness. It is all summed up in what Jesus desires for His disciples: 'Be ye therefore perfect, even as your Father in heaven is perfect.' If Christ be formed in us, as Paul prayed might be true of his converts, then the world inside becomes richly furnished with His gifts, freely given though obtained for us 'at such tremendous cost'. Our testimony will therefore point always to the donor, for we have nothing to reveal which has not been given and nothing which we have earned, merited or deserved. All is of God, grace and faith are His gifts by which we are saved, and as we

draw aside the veil of that inner life we remind ourselves as we reveal to others the abiding truth: 'O to
grace how great a debtor, daily I'm constrained to be.'
Jesus called His first disciples to be witnesses to these
mighty acts of God – historic facts – in His plan and
purpose for our salvation, but they were also to witness
through 'repentance and remission of sins' their effects
in human hearts. The Gospels abound in examples of
changed lives, and whenever the good news of His
redeeming grace has been received the word has been
confirmed 'by the miracles that followed' (Mark 16.20,
N.E.B.). The finest argument, then and now, because it
is unanswerable, is 'the miracle of the changed life'
(the title of one of the earliest sermons I tried to preach).
Personal evangelism is therefore an intimate expression
of what Christ has done and is doing for me.

Here is a perfect illustration of personal evangelism
in two sentences from the answer of a young man being
examined orally as a candidate for the Methodist
ministry to a question about how he became a Christian.
'I was greatly helped by a fellow workman in an
engineering shop. I saw God in my mate and that
friend led me to the experience of salvation.' That was
the Apostolic way, as Paul writes: 'And they glorified
God in me' (Galatians 1.24, A.V.). We are the only
Gospel most men read, our daily lives are 'living
epistles'. Good works can bring glory to God as Jesus
declared (Matthew 5.16). *All* loving service *in His name*
can be used of God to bring men and women to a
knowledge and acceptance of His will. 'In His name'
distinguishes Christian service from secular social
service, though God can and does bless both forms. It
is objective because it points to God's acts in Jesus
Christ for us and our salvation, and it is subjective

because it relates them to my personal knowledge and experience of the wonderful gifts appropriated by faith with thanksgiving. Nothing is more convincing in speech than authentic, personal experience. Is the lack of this the explanation of the paucity of personal testimony? If the inner domain of the soul is sparsely furnished, there would seem little point in drawing aside the curtain! The outer life, as I wrote earlier, reflects the inner world and perhaps this is the explanation of the lack of difference between many of us who profess the Christian faith and those who are not yet Christians. Have we experienced the difference that makes all the difference? The difference when the Holy Spirit through Christ changes the house within into His dwelling place. That vital difference made so real on the day of Pentecost, when each follower of our Lord, whether man or woman, could have said: 'I live, yet not I, but Christ liveth in me.' This is the experience which makes a Christian a convinced and convincing witness. There is no substitute for this first-hand, personal, vital relationship and experience of Christ. 'We have heard with our ears, our fathers have told us . . .' wrote the Psalmist, that is tradition ('opinions and ideas passed on from one generation to another, *unwritten*') and it is good, but not good enough. Its inadequacy is exposed in the searching question put by Jesus in reply to Pilate's testimony: 'Sayest thou this of thyself or did others tell it thee of me?'

'To know Him . . .' not just to know about Him or of Him is fundamental to effective Christian witness. 'I know whom I have believed' is the heart of the Christian's creed and message. Christ is the good news of the evangelist, all He has done, all He desires to do, and all He will do for all who accept Him. To all such is given this further knowledge that 'it is God which worketh in you both to will and to do of his good pleasure'. It is of God's work in our souls we are called to speak. Yet as Phillips Brooks said of preaching, so also of personal witness for Christ, it is 'truth mediated through personality'. Scripture affords, as often, the most helpful illustration. Think of Paul in his glorious personal testimony before Festus and King Agrippa (Acts 26). Rudely interrupted – so it seems to me – by the loud voice of Festus declaring that the Apostle must be mad, Paul did not lose his temper, but politely rebutted the statement and appealed to the King to confirm the truth of his witness, claiming that he would believe the prophetic setting of his declaration. To which the King replied: 'Almost thou persuadest me to be a Christian.' Whether the King said it sincerely or, as I believe, from a quickened conscience, Paul's immediate response was: 'I would to God that not only thou, but also all who hear me this day were both almost and altogether such as I am, except these bonds.' Paul said it to a very mixed company, and we may therefore infer that God can make a Christian of anyone but what exactly did Paul mean? 'I wish you were of such a righteous character as I am?' or 'I wish you all spoke the sober truth that I do?' – surely not, for the language of the prisoner, as we know, was 'I, the least of the apostles', and 'I, the chief of sinners'. What he meant was: 'I do not wish you were handcuffed as I am, but I wish with all my soul that you knew within, as a personal experience, the peace, joy, freedom, purpose and power of a life constrained by the love of Christ.' 'Make me a captive, Lord, and then I shall be free', was the proved experience of Paul, a bond-slave of Jesus Christ.

I remember many years ago sitting opposite to a stranger travelling on the same train south from Newcastle. We read our newspapers without exchanging a word until well south of York. Then I made an opening remark and in a very few minutes discovered he was a South African farmer on a visit to this country. Being an agriculturist myself I was, of course, keenly interested, so put the simple question: 'What's life like in your country?' Then the floodgates opened and I could hardly get a word in as he was carried away in an eloquent description of farming and life in his own country.

Two men stood one day with a group of people listening to an open-air speaker, a carpenter's son of Nazareth. When he had finished and went on his way, they shyly followed. 'Then Jesus turned and saw them following, and saith unto them, What seek ye? They said unto him, Rabbi (which is interpreted, Master), where dwellest thou? He saith unto them, Come and see.' I imagine it would take them but a few minutes to reach his temporary place of abode, but it was after months of living with him in the inner circle of the chosen Twelve that they discovered increasingly the wonder of the world in which He dwelt and longed to live in it themselves. How powerfully and irresistibly were they attracted by His inner world of perfect trust in the Father, of consecration to the will of God with all its consequent blessings, of ability to meet every emergency and extremity of need in himself and in others, of love which healed and grace which transformed and insight which could recognize God and realize His Presence everywhere. In due course they, and so many others to whom they bore their witness, were united as Peter said: 'to show forth the praises of him who hath called you out of darkness into his marvellous light' (1 Peter 2.9.), or as Paul declared of Christ's work to the Christians at Colosse, 'Who hath delivered us from the power of darkness and hath translated us into the kingdom of his dear Son' (Colossians 1.13). How dark the inner world of self subject to the dictatorship of a sinful nature can become! How light, and therefore how joyful and wholesome, life can be when the Light of the World is the centre of my inner world! It was Evelyn Underhill who wrote of the 'utter delightfulness of the consecrated life'.

Two things, at least, may be said of the inner world transformed by the Indwelling Presence of Christ. (1) It is a world of ever-enlarging horizons of possibility, for it is a libel of the Christian faith to say that it makes life narrow, cabinned or confined. I know it is a narrow way trod by the minority but, paradoxically the deepest and widest experience of life. The real Christian experience enobles every virtue, enriches every activity, widens our interests, intensifies and enriches personality and is the source of the highest and finest culture. God forgive us if we have misrepresented the Christian life as something which maims, impoverishes or impairs life. It is a denial of self but not of fullness of life. It has the promise of the finest life here in the pilgrimage of the years with issues, promises and hopes which run out beyond the frontier of time into eternity.

(2) It is therefore a world of eternal blessedness. The Christian is not 'rushed for time' – he has come to terms with it, as Jesus did. 'I must do the work of Him that hath sent me while it is day, the night cometh when no man can work' – that is here. Here in what Keats described as 'this vale of soul making', we enjoy a foretaste of life beyond time and death. Truly 'Thou

hast set my feet in a large place'. Christians are *en route* for their eternal home. 'There's your ticket for heaven, Mother', said the somewhat facetious official to the applicant for the Old Age Pension as he handed her the authorized document. 'Not exactly that,' she replied, 'but it will make the waiting-room a bit more pleasant, thank you.'

It is in daily conduct and unpremeditated conversation that we reveal the splendour of that world found in time but not bound by it, in which we live in Christ. The chief method of personal evangelism is then to live the Gospel, and in so doing challenge explanation, arouse curiosity and awaken need and desire. 'All are yours; and ye are Christ's, and Christ is God's' (1 Corinthians 3.22, 23). There are no millionaires to be compared with those who are filled with the limitless riches of Christ. 'And O that my Saviour were your Saviour, too,' is the prayer longing which makes possible the Holy Spirit's guidance on any and every method whereby we may bring to others the good news and joyful experience of God in Christ.

There is no one method, and somehow, to me, the word technique seems out of place, though fishing is a craft and a personal evangelist is called to be a fisher of men. Rather would I try to summarize, at the end of this chapter, certain essentials which interpenetrate most personal interviews and conversations in winning souls for Christ. Before doing so I would simply enumerate what I have found indispensable *material* equipment: (*a*) a room, preferably in your own or other's home enabling a private talk, (*b*) a prayer folder file for notes of persons for whom you pray regularly, (*c*) a prayer book for names and addresses of those who make a decision for Christ and wish you to remember them, (d) a decision card and suitable literature helpful to future progress in prayers, Bible Study, witness and service – in short the use of the means of grace whereby he can *grow* in grace.

(1) Seek to bring home to your enquirer his need, whether it be that of a young person carrying 'the burden of the unexpressed', or of the more common knowledge of what has been expressed that brings regret, shame and remorse. A sense of inner defeat, frustration, moral and spiritual failure, estrangement from God, are needs not uncommonly revealed in personal interviews. Whatever may be the realized need, all need forgiveness, the power to overcome temptation and a right relationship with God.

(2) Help him to realize that his highest hopes and dreams can only be attained by acknowledging his failure and helplessness and then placing his trust in Christ who not only can save *from* but also *to* the uttermost.

(3) Declare Christ's offer to be what every man needs, namely a Friend, a Guide and a Saviour. That need should be distinguished from want, for all of us at times want what we do not need, and need what we do not want. Stress our supreme need, which is to *believe* in Jesus.

(4) Challenge him to make up his mind – no one else can do it. No one can act in this matter by proxy. 'Choose you this day whom you will serve' for 'no man can serve two masters'. A Christian counsellor, having lovingly, prayerfully examined with an enquirer, the evidence for and against acceptance of Christ, makes clear, at the right moment, that the challenge of an encounter with Christ is to come to a verdict. 'What shall I do then with Jesus which is called Christ?'

Pause in silence to listen to what He says. This 'quiet time' does not necessarily mean closing one's eyes.

(5) This in turn may lead to prayer for and with the seeker, and it is all the better if the latter will himself ask in simple, natural, personal words what he desires Christ to give him. Hence the prayer – simple yet profound – which was silently prayed by the counsellor at the beginning before the interview may well be the most fitting audible prayer at the close by the one now desirous of becoming a Christian, namely: 'Lord, what wilt thou have me to do?'

(6) After commitment or re-commitment of the soul to Christ, there is always the next step in the right direction. 'He made as though He would go further' – He is always doing that. Always encourage the new convert to pray and look for that next step, and when it is seen and known, to obey. It may be personal witness, reparation, reconciliation with someone else, diligence and discipline in using the means of grace, recognizing that he will do all things and think all things from then onwards as in His sight. Ask for a promise that this will be his continuing quest to enable him to confess Christ before others through personal witness.

(7) Impress upon him that acceptance in Christ is not dependent upon our feelings but upon His sure and unfailing promises, and that faith fulfils itself in faithfulness to Him who will be with him always.

(8) Warn him that temptations will be his lot to the end of his days, but the more he is tested, the more he can prove God's power by dependence upon God.

(9) Give him the best yardstick of spiritual progress which is increasing dependence upon God.

(10) Encourage him to seek increasing consecration

to God's will, which will result in God having the last word in *everything* he chooses or decides, for 'in His will is our peace', and when we know and do that, all will be well with our souls, whatever happens.

It remains to be said that only as a personal evangelist seeks increasingly for himself to know God, to know people, to know the way of prayer and to know the Word of God, can he become the instrument in God's hands for the winning of souls. The more he becomes knowledgeable in the deep things of God the more effectively will the Holy Spirit be able to use him to reach 'the hidden depths of many a heart'. He must seek an increasing experience of God only then like Jesus, our blessed example and God's pioneer personal evangelist shall we be able to say, 'We speak of what we know' (John 3.11, N.E.B.).

CHAPTER SEVEN

THE MESSENGERS

'How beautiful are the feet of them that preach the gospel of peace, and bring glad tidings of good things'
(Romans 10.15, from Isaiah 52.7).

IN MY EARLIER days, I often heard my father, a Methodist minister, speak in admiration of the Rev. Charles Garrett, a great evangelist. Recently I heard the Rev. Cyril E. Gwyther speak of a reply Garrett once made at a Convention in Liverpool when the well-known American evangelist, Dwight Moody, turned to Garrett and said: 'Tell them how to reach the masses for Christ.' Garret's reply consisted of three words: 'Go to them.' 'Go ye into all the world,' said Jesus, and it means just that – 'Go to them', in their homes, factories, places of business, and haunts of pleasure and recreation. Hence the blessedness of the *feet*, and the prayer we so often sing too glibly without realizing the cost: 'Take my feet and let them be swift and beautiful for Thee.' 'For unless we can first reach those we hope to win then all our evangelism is in vain', writes one of the wisest of divinely inspired instructors in evangelism, Dr D. P. Thomson.

Years ago I took part in a large demonstration with several platforms in Hyde Park, London. A photograph in my personal album shows that famous preacher, Dr W. E. Sangster, speaking from Platform 2, of which

I was chairman, with its description 'The Message of Modern Methodism' – 'Personal, Social, National and International'. Our slogan was 'Methodism goes to the People'. Returning that night by sleeper to Newcastle-upon-Tyne, I woke before dawn and lay awake reflecting on our witness in Hyde Park. I hoped and prayed that it had served God's purpose, when suddenly I realized that within a few hours some 700,000 Methodist Christians, myself included, would be 'going to the people', and how many more Christians in other regiments of the Army of Christ would be doing the same, I could only imagine. The all-important question was would they be messengers of good things, of the best things, the gospel of peace and of glad tidings?

After the *enlightened* mind and the *warmed* heart which Christ brought to the two sad disciples whom He met on the road from Jerusalem to Emmaus, 'and as He sat at meat with them', came that personal knowledge – 'and they knew Him' – which transformed them and their whole outlook upon life. Then came the culminating blessing of the *willing* feet. 'They rose up the same hour and returned to Jerusalem and found the eleven gathered together, and them that were with them. . . . And they told what things were done in the way and how he was known of them in breaking of bread.' Thus Luke reports in what George Eliot described as the most beautiful story in all the world, found in the final chapter of his Gospel. 'And as they thus spake' – more excitingly translated by James Moffatt: 'Just as they were speaking' – 'Jesus himself stood in the midst of them, and said unto them, Peace be unto you.' Surely the first of countless confirmations of Mark's testimony in the last verse of his Gospel: 'the Lord working with them and confirming the word with signs ("miracles" N.E.B.) following'. Messengers – plural – for this is no 'do it yourself' project. Always the personal evangelist in action finds the Presence of Christ and is assured of the guidance and inspiration of the Holy Spirit. Moreover in house-to-house visitation there is much to be said, as I know from long experience, for going in twos, as did the seventy messengers sent out by Jesus in His earthly ministry. This is an ideal field for ecumenical co-operation and always worth while.

Every day, then, a personal evangelist goes forth as a King's Messenger. 'Sent out by the Holy Spirit' (Acts 13.4, R.S.V.). He not only goes with us but He prepares the way for us. In his fine book on preaching, *With Ardour and Accuracy*, Dr Leonard Small tells of Principal Martin saying to his students: 'Gentlemen, when you are going about your pastoral duties, you will often find yourself outside a door or ringing a bell, wishing it might not open because behind the door lies some situation of sin, suffering or sorrow with which you feel incompetent to deal. When you feel like that always remind yourself that Christ is behind that door already and at work. All you have to do is to make real His Presence and His Power.' The same applies to both ministers and laymen who engage in personal evangelism. It is said of F. D. Maurice, that great theologian and founder of the Christian Socialist Movement in this country, that he believed Christ had redeemed all men, whether they believed in Him or not. It is our work to persuade men to accept and appropriate the blessing of reconciliation with God which is theirs by virtue of the atoning sacrifice of Christ. The prayer to the Holy Spirit: 'O plead the truth and make reply to every argument of sin' we find answered again and again. Each day a Christian after morning prayer goes from God, with God, for God into his vocation (wherever God has placed him) to speak the truth *in love* with his life and lips. 'Evangelism in Depth' has been described by one of its able exponents as taking the seed to the soil rather than bringing the soil to the seed.

It was Somerset Maugham who, describing Balzac's gift as a writer in envisaging men in their relation to one another and in relation to the world they live in, wrote: 'You go to the barber's to get your hair cut; it means nothing to you, but because of some casual remark of yours it may be a turning point in the barber's life. . . . By realizing all that this implies Balzac was able to give a vivid and exciting impression of the multifariousness of life, its confusions and cross purposes and of the remoteness of *the causes that result in significant effects*' (the italics are mine). Did not Jesus say: 'I tell you on the day of judgement men will render account for every careless word they utter' (Matthew 12.36, R.S.V.)? Even more challenging are His words in the previous verse: 'For a man's words depend upon what fills his heart' (Phillips). What immeasurable blessing can be released to the world through men and women in any and every walk of life who walk and talk with Christ daily and who are thus given the grace, wisdom guidance and power to speak a personal word for Him. Think of the actual result which came out of a personal word from John Henry Jowitt's Sunday School teacher, who met him on the day before the articles were to be signed for Jowitt to enter a Halifax firm of solicitors to be an articled clerk. 'Jowitt,' writes his biographer, 'met his Sunday School teacher by accident, and told him of his decision.' 'I had always hoped that you would

go into the ministry', said Mr Dewhirst, the Sunday
School teacher, looking grieved. This simple sentence
led ultimately to Jowitt becoming a minister, known
on both sides of the Atlantic as 'the Prince of Preachers'.
It was the same with Mr Kimball, another Sunday
School teacher, who in obedience to the Holy Spirit
(let us drop the words good impulse, and say rather
the call of God) went one weekday into the back of
a boot store to speak to a young man of the Sunday
School. 'I found Moody in the back part of the building,
wrapping up shoes. I went up to him at once and putting
my hands on his shoulder I made what I afterwards
felt was a very weak plea for Christ. I don't know just
what words I used, nor could Mr Moody tell. I simply
told him of Christ's love for him and the love Christ
wanted in return. That was all there was. It seemed
the young man was just ready for the light that then
broke upon him, and there in the back of that store in
Boston, he gave himself and his life to Christ.' Can anyone of us attempt to measure the influence of what we
say to others day by day, or *what we fail to say*? And it
is not just by accident that we meet them. A few words
spoken for Christ can mean *the* turning point in another
life.

'Be not conformed to this world', but we all do tend
to conform, *especially in conversation*, hence Paul's further
challenge: 'to see that our conduct (N.E.B.) and conversation (A.V.) be worthy of the Gospel of Christ.'
If we are men and women on a mission in the everyday
world, messengers with a message of vital importance
to ourselves and every man, commissioned by one whom
we love most and believing in the promise that it shall
be given us what we are to say, then naturally, rele-
vantly, convincingly and lovingly, the word of God will

come through our conversation. Lives wholly dedicated to God are constantly inspired (inbreathed) by the Spirit of God. 'A man's conversation', writes that eminent medical authority, Lord Brain, 'is more revealing than any description of him and may tell us more about him than his own formal writing.' If that be so, and who am I to doubt it? then how often do I consciously and unconsciously show that Christ means everything to me – yes, everything? One recalls the B.B.C. 'First Impressions' and the panel which had to decide the person hidden from their sight by the answers they gave – via the voice of the compère – to their questions. I once adopted and adapted it for my Fellowship, putting the following questions which members were asked to answer as honestly and naturally as possible.

1. Church-going is to me . . .
2. So far as Sunday is concerned, I . . .
3. Total abstinence is to me . . .
4. Can you conceive of a condition in your life in which it would be true to say 'I've lost everything?'
5. When I am depressed, I . . .
6. It's my belief that . . .
7. If I hear of someone who has spoken critically behind my back, I . . .
8. What are the sins which delay the coming of a better world?
9. I wish I could . . .
10. My greatest ambition is . . .

The answers given were interesting, challenging and also revealing. They served to show how human we are and to what extent we were really like Christ.

Above all, how impossible it ought to be if we are really Christian to conceal it.

Yet, by what we don't say, how often we misrepresent our Christian faith, and how often because we forget His constant Presence with us do we miss the opportunity to witness in our conversation to the value of prayer, for example. 'I thought afterwards I ought to have said . . .' 'I missed a chance of saying . . .' 'How I wish I had thought of saying . . .' are common enough experiences and impressions of Christian people. Much is being said, thought and arranged in Church circles these days about the training of laymen for churchmanship and the outreach work of the church. Such training is needful, but the question arises how eager are church people to be trained? It depends on the extent to which we realize our privilege and reponsibility as messengers of the good news. 'Proclaim the message, press it home on all occasions' (2 Timothy 4.2, N.E.B.). We should not wait until we feel like speaking it but when we know we ought to do so.

Lest any reader should think I am overemphasizing the importance of the spoken witness, let me repeat that what you are will speak louder than what you say. Matthew Arnold declared that conduct was fourfifths of life. I am sure Beatrice Cleland is right in her wonderful words which I have beside me, printed on a beautiful card, as follows:

Indwelt

Not merely by the words you say,
Not only in your deeds confessed
But in the most unconscious way
Is CHRIST expressed.

Is it a beatific smile?
A holy light upon your brow?
Oh, no – I felt HIS presence while
You laughed just now.

For me 'twas not the truth you taught,
To you so clear, to me still dim,
But when you came to me you brought
A sense of HIM.

And from your eyes HE beckons me
And from your heart HIS love is shed,
Till I lose sight of you, and see
The CHRIST instead.

Yet by 'the words you say' you express the Christ within, and in their absence how greatly the cause of Christ can suffer.

I remember speaking on behalf of the 'Religion and Life' Movement, and introducing my address with the remark that my only criticism of the Movement was the description. The religion I humbly represented was more truly entitled: 'Religion is Life', and therefore should not be a neglected topic in daily conversation and only talked about in churches or religious meetings. 'Certainly one would suppose that anyone genuinely holding a religious belief would regard this as the most important thing in life, and far from seeking to conceal it, would wish to proclaim it from the housetops' (Barbara Wootton in *In a World I Never Made*). Religion and Politics are subjects which are often banned because they are regarded as controversial, and to be reticent about spiritual experience is sometimes regarded as good manners. Yet how voluble people can be in talking about other things, ailments, holidays, TV features, fashions, etc., or of themselves! Propaganda is now a 'dirty' word, but it is a good gardening word meaning to propagate or multiply, and advertisement which can be dishonest and evil can also be useful and beneficial. The early Christians used the spoken word as they went from 'house to house', we are told in the Acts of the Apostles. The publication *Time and Tide* carried in a panel these words: 'We do not mind what you say – but talk about *Time and Tide*.' Blackpool landladies, I have read, receive free tickets to certain shows, films, etc., because of their propaganda value in recommending to visitors what they ought to see. The Bible contains the good news of the Gospel of God's redeeming love and purpose for His children whereby we can share in His fellowship and power, but so few of our fellow countrymen ever read the Bible. Human lips and lives must bring the good news to the world. 'According to my Gospel' was Paul's testimony, and it must be the same for the twentieth-century Christian if the good news is to reach those in 'Christian' England who never read a Bible or go to a church (except to be given a Christian name and some day to be buried, in both cases being carried there).

After all, it was Jesus Himself who said, 'Ye shall be witnesses unto me', and normally a witness is called to testify in speech. 'We speak that we do know and testify that we have seen.' Evidence by hearsay is disallowed, or at least discounted. The witness who arrests attention in a court of law says: 'I was there when it happened.' Can it be that we lack first-hand knowledge of God in Christ and so are weak in spoken witness? When the Old Testament writer said: 'Would that all the Lord's people were prophets', he did not mean he wished they were all able to say what would happen in future (our common inadequate interpretation of the word prophecy). All prophecy is of God and His prophets are those who forth tell – which can include foretell—what God has said to them or done for them. They witness to the truth as it has been revealed to them. A fine example of a witness for Christ is found in the man who those about him knew had been blind from his birth, when he declared: 'One thing I know, that whereas I was blind, now I see' (John 9.25). It is thrilling to think of the unfolding wonder of life which would come to this man from the moment he received his sight. Is not this miracle a parable of the Christian life? Is it not true of those who are brought out of spiritual darkness into His most marvellous light that 'Lord, I was blind, I could not see'? And has not life become increasingly glorious as we have walked with him whom John declared as the Light of men? If this is not my experience as a Christian, is it because I am no longer an active messenger? 'Where is the blessedness I knew when first I saw the Lord?' is never the question of a Christian loyal to our Lord's command to go and make Christians and if we obey, then we can claim the promise: 'Lo, I am with you always.'

We not only keep but we enlarge and enrich what we have of Christian experience by sharing it with others. As we tell others what we know and possess of the truth as it is in Jesus, we receive as much, some would say more, than we give. Every teacher knows that we best retain what we give to others. A growing and glowing experience of Christ is the reward of those who continue faithful in personal evangelism. The messenger becomes increasingly sure of the glorious message he has to declare and assured of the abiding companionship of the Lord who commissioned him. Personal evangelism is never a question I repeat of 'do it yourself.' 'Go and do' is the command and conditional promise of His presence with us.

Then why are we so neglectful of our personal mission, and in consequence lose the spiritual glow? Is the Bible answer a clue when it speaks of being 'afraid of men's faces'? Don't we need to pray that we may lose self consciousness in Christ's consciousness? Is it really true that we refrain from speaking about spiritual matters because we fear embarrassing the other person? Or is it that we fear embarrassing ourselves? There were those who believed in Christ in New Testament days but did not avow Him, and the reason is given: they placed public opinion and personal popularity higher than the approval of God. It is so easy to sing: 'I'm not ashamed to own my Lord or to defend His cause' in a Christian rally and to let the cause of Christ go by default in the office, shop, factory, school, university, with our neighbours or where we work and walk by our silence. A Christian is 'a voice through which Christ speaks'. Paul's description of a Christian is one who believes in the Risen Christ and 'confesses with his lips' that Jesus is Lord. The same word is used by Jesus when He says: 'Whosoever therefore shall confess me before men him will I confess also before my Father which is in heaven.' The Annual Covenant Service 'which has been a fruitful source of blessing to Methodism ever since 1755' contains these words in the form of service in the prayers of Confession. 'Forgive us, we beseech Thee . . . our hesitating witness for Christ', to which all taking part respond with the words: 'Have mercy upon us and forgive us, O Lord.'

Proverbially we say: 'He who hesitates is lost' – it is certainly true of so many opportunities for vocal witness and surely we ought to add to the prayer just quoted: 'and help us to overcome our hesitancy and fear.'

The matter became personal for me very many years ago when one evening, in reviewing the day before, kneeling to say my last prayers, I recalled an incident at coffee in the University Union that morning. A 'dirty' story had been told, several laughed. I did not laugh but remained silent. I began, as I recall, that moment to find reasons for my attitude. I was a junior member of staff; my silent witness surely was the best way and so on, until I realized all such reasons were excuses not reasons. I am so thankful now that I went down on my knees with sincere repentance in my heart. I knew what I should have done and how I could have said in a gracious way what I ought to have said. I prayed more earnestly than ever before to confess His presence in my life and therefore to remember that He was with me always in every circumstance or experience. I waited for His word of forgiveness and equally for His word of promise and power. I shall never forget that night, for I began to find then an increasing desire and freedom to confess Him before both staff colleagues and students in the University. 'Not as if I had already attained or were already perfect', but at least those with whom I worked knew, and know, where I stand, and I continue to ask Him to make me, in conversation and conduct, in behaviour and service for others, a more faithful ambassador.

For never should we forget that one day an ambassador for Christ is recalled and translated to the higher service. One day he will stand before the King of Kings, and Lord of Lords. All the King's Messengers will have to give an account, though each for himself at His appointed time. Every Christian is entrusted with the Gospel. He is a trustee of the Christian heritage. We shall be asked to give an account of how we have acted as stewards of what Phillips translates as 'the magnificently varied grace of God'. Hence Charles Wesley, whose hymns are so clearly Scriptural, bid us pray in one of his verses:

> *Arm me with jealous care,*
> *As in Thy sight to live,*
> *And O Thy servant, Lord, prepare*
> *A strict account to give.*

That day of all days will come for you and me, we know not when but come it will. 'Blessed', said Jesus, 'is that servant whom his lord when he cometh shall find so doing' – that is, as Jesus said, 'that faithful and wise steward' who fulfilled his lord's appointment and will. Happy indeed are those who when they see Him face to face, because of His mercy and their faithfulness are able to look upon His face and not be ashamed. It will not be a matter of how much we have been used of God to win for Christ, but how faithfully we have sought to sow the seed and reap the harvest through personal evangelism. By this is meant how much we tried, depending on His help, to mediate the love of God to men and women, wherever they are and of whatever colour or clime, and therefore, on the interpretation of the word neighbour in the story of the Good Samaritan, to people in need. So all caring in His Name and for His sake contributes to the pattern of evangelism, food for the hungry, a cup of cold water to the thirsty, clothes for the naked, prison visitation.

God can bless to the end that His love can be made real and His Name glorified.

Caring, sharing and *daring* are characteristics of the Christian Messenger, and how blessed, then, are the feet of a courier of Christ who brings 'Glad tidings of good things'. Blessings for others and God's blessing on himself are the joyful accompaniment of such dedicated service. I cannot repeat too often that this is both the desire and will of Christ for all His followers. With varying gifts we can complement each other by dedicating what we have and are to this supreme vocation of service. The crowning reward is His verdict on our stewardship in time: 'Well done, good and faithful servant.'

'If I had a brother or sister that I loved, degraded in the East End, I should not rest till I had done my utmost to save him, and others would think that that was only to be expected of me; but I *have* thousands of brothers and sisters there and I calmly let them be' – (quoted from *Margaret Ethel Macdonald*, by J. Ramsay Macdonald). Should I not feel the same and even more so about the spiritual as well as the physical needs of God's children? If sin is, as I believe, the malignant disease of the soul and I have the message of healing and health (wholeness and holiness), should I not 'give and give and give again what God hath given thee', as Studdert Kennedy put it, of my knowledge of the cure.

Christ can use everyone and every gift consecrated to Him to bring someone into the personal knowledge of His love, if we give ourselves to Him and, like Him, give ourselves to others.

> *O use me, Lord, use even me,*
> *Just as Thou wilt, and when, and where.*

No one ever prayed that prayer regularly, and meant it, who did not receive the answer in the power and presence of Him who said, and continues to say: 'Follow me and I will make you fishers of men.' Ask for the power of the Holy Spirit to fill your life and then remember that Christian discipleship is always faith and obedience.

If what you have read thus far in these pages moves you to begin, or to begin again, to share your faith and experience in Christ with those who do not know Him personally, then be on your guard against the temptation just to feel the desire, or worse still, to repress it. Do something about it – and *do it now*. The first contact we can make with unconverted people is on our knees, the second on our feet, the third with words, whether written or spoken (though often both). Dr Sangster used to keep on his prayer desk, beside his Bible, hymn book, etc., a plain exercise book with the page headed for each day: ACTION. My friend both spoke and listened to God when he prayed and would write down God's guiding directions. 'I do it', he said, 'because it saves me from indulging in feelings which never become facts.' Ask then for a message and power to become a messenger and then *go into action*.

CHAPTER EIGHT

MEETING POINT

'*And he saith unto them, Follow me, and I will make you fishers of men.*'   Matthew 4.19.

YEARS AGO I was privileged to be a member of Dr W. E. Sangster's team for the Schools of Evangelism he led at different centres throughout the country. The subject he usually allotted to me was 'How to lead another soul to Christ' – and more than once, when in briefing the team he came to me, he would say: 'Be sure, Cecil, to tell them *how*.' Specific lay-training in personal evangelism for those received into church membership and refresher courses in the same, I am convinced, would be blessed of God. In this final chapter I want to try to gather up our thinking on this vitally important question in some practical conclusions with examples of the personal evangelist *in action*.

How, then, can I convert someone? Well, the first thing to be said is that you can't and I can't, but what we can do is to be used by the Holy Spirit to bring someone to that decision which makes possible conversion. Let God use your words and life to this end. Pray that you may not get in the way of the Holy Spirit. When you have done all He desires leave it to Him to further His own work and continue in your prayers to believe that He will always distinguish between decision, conversion, re-conversion and re-dedication. All is of God and the Holy Spirit is the One who convicts of sin and need, converts and consecrates, inspires and renders effective the words and work of a personal evangelist. The word given to me by an old saint of God when I first began to preach, namely: 'Honour the Holy Spirit' is the first priority in personal evangelism. It follows, therefore, that the task of winning another person for Christ must be begun, continued and ended in prayer. Begin in your daily private prayers to pray for unconverted friends and associates. In the People Next Door movement, held in the first part of 1967 for all denominations, members of the groups were asked to make contact preferably with a non-churchgoer with whom to discuss the findings of each group meeting. In a subsequent conference held at Swanwick to discuss the results of P.N.D., the *New Christian* for July 13th, 1967, reports 'one of the horrifying facts that emerged was that many church people did not know anyone outside'. I have wondered whether those who did make such contacts have followed them up in subsequent months. Over the years I have sometimes been led to ask the members of my Weekly Christian Fellowship Group to write down, after a time of quiet prayer, the names or description of a few people they met regularly, say every two or three weeks, of whom they were doubtful whether they were committed Christians. In my own list, I once wrote the man who invariably cuts my hair at a well-known store in Newcastle; the man who was then employed as a street cleaner and whom I often greeted with 'Good morning' and a remark about the weather; a blind man whom I often noticed used a seat in a sunny place in the next road to that in which my own home is situated, and so on. Archbishop Temple has a word in one of his books that if we pray for any particular virtue, whether it be patience or courage or love, one of the answers is that God gives to us the opportunity for exercising that virtue. For example, if I pray for courage to witness, an opportunity will come for me to be in part the answer to my prayer. Thus, having prayed for unconverted friends, we must ask God to enable us to stand by our prayers. 'Pray on every occasion in the power of the Spirit. To this end keep watch and persevere . . .' writes the Apostle Paul in Ephesians 6.18. (N.E.B.). Hear above all our blessed Lord, as He prayed: 'For their sakes I consecrate myself, that they also may be consecrated through the truth', which surely means I offer myself for the answering of my prayer.

Certain words are rarely in my vocabulary, such as 'good impulse', 'coincidence', 'chance' and never at all the word 'luck'. If we believe in His guidance and if by His grace we are made clean and holy, then we shall know how true it is that 'the steps of a good man are ordered by the Lord', which means detailed and continuous guidance. How often I have been led to pray for someone whom I have not seen for some time, and whom I feel God desires me to help and, sometimes by letter or not infrequently within days, a personal unexpected encounter has confirmed the inner bidding of the Spirit. In this, as in so many other ways, we err not because of ignorance of God's desire and will but through disobedience.

Contact can lead to conversation and in time (God's time) to confidence in your power to understand, to help, to counsel. Living a prayer*ful* life each day, we can ask for the Spirit's guidance to speak the right word at the right time, and for that aliveness and alertness which enables us to recognize the right opportunity. Few are likely to find a man reading his Bible as he journeyed, as Philip did, who after a question was able 'to preach unto him, Jesus', but the Christian Gospel is never irrelevant though we can be. We once started a group in the University which I was privileged to lead, called the 'No Name Group', which included several avowed atheists, some agnostics and a few Christians. No subject was debarred from discussion, hence artificial insemination, abortion, free love, all manner of subjects were freely considered. The only condition made, and willingly accepted, was five minutes at the end, in which I was allowed to sum up the Christian attitude or case. I never found this was impossible, relying wholly as I did on the promise, 'Do not begin worrying about how you will conduct your defence or what you will say. For when the time comes the Holy Spirit will instruct you what to say' (Luke 12.12, N.E.B.). There is, of course, both a right and a wrong interpretation of what it means to rely on the Spirit. Only as we seek continually to be better informed Christians by study of the Word, prayerful meditation on its application and implications to our life in the world can we know His abiding inspiration at every turn. There is both a theology and a practice of personal evangelism.

No Christian is denied the joy of personal evangelism, for every Christian can pray for others, and how often the prayer of the personal evangelist is increased in effectiveness by the fellowship of a prayer group.

There are two arts – and art I define as the best way of doing the right thing – which God can develop and use in the work of the personal evangelist. The first is that of understanding listening to the person you seek to win by your witness for Christ. Beginning, as I have said, where they are, and being patient if at times what is said seems irrelevant, superficial and beside the point, the Holy Spirit will guide as to the second art, that of speaking the timely word which leads to that confession of need, desire, disquietude, enabling that same Spirit to take full control of the situation. There is no one approach, for no two persons are alike, each one has travelled a different road in the inner life of knowledge and experience. Whilst there are many ways into the Kingdom, in the end they narrow down to a sense of need; only then can Christ become real to anyone. Always it was a sense of need that brought Christ to men and men to Christ in the Gospel records which resulted in the faith that made possible His miracles of grace. Because this need is met so wonder-fully and so completely in Christ's finished work on the Cross, the message of the Cross is crucial and central to the witness of the evangelist. The title of a book I once saw is true of the conversation and counsel of the personal evangelist: *All Roads Lead to Calvary*. It is at the Cross that men see the light of God's redeeming love most clearly and their own unworthiness and need for His forgiveness. All talk, then, of being as good as this or that other person, or that betrayal and denial such as Judas and Peter committed have nothing to do with me, are seen not only as unbefitting but as self deceit. Only as we find forgiveness at the Cross do we find life – as George Matheson described it, 'life that shall endless be'. Nothing can be as important in life as this personal encounter with Christ. 'He died that we might be forgiven, He died to make us good.' So I would repeat that only 'Repentance toward God and trust in Jesus Christ' brings salvation from sin and spiritual death.

Evangelism brings the message of God's love by service to the hungry and homeless and hopeless, and in proclaiming the good news of God's purpose and plan for the individual and for community life for the nation and the world. 'The most important and productive missionary work of all', said Dr John R. Mott, one of the greatest Christian leaders of this century, 'is that of relating men one by one through reasonable and vital faith to Jesus Christ. This is the crowning work, the most highly multiplying work, the most enduring work.'

After all, most of our life is a matter of personal relationships, and a personal evangelist is mainly concerned with bringing men and women, one by one, into a right relationship to God and with their fellow men. This includes his environment, for new men in Christ no longer recognize the distinction between sacred and secular, but seek to use and fashion all things for the glory of God who created all things to this end.

The personal evangelist is often charged with oversimplifying the complex issues of the world in which we live today. Yet the plain fact is that better politics can only come through better politicians and better people, and the same applies to other areas of thought and life. It is remarkable how often the direct, personal, courageous approach to what seems a complex problem can reduce if not always resolve its complexity and inspire others to take action. There is much wisdom in Pepys's remark in his famous diary: 'Nobody beginning, I did.'

Much is made in these days of the need for new words and ways to express the Gospel in our age, and

I recognize the need for re-thinking of the faith in contemporary conditions, but love is a universally understood language. The Christlike life (which is the meaning of holiness) commends the Gospel in a language which needs no translation. Even a child can respond to the love that gave all on the Cross. 'Thou gav'st Thyself for me, I give myself to Thee.' The unique gift intrusted to us to offer to others is Jesus Christ. This is the meeting point between earth and heaven, the sinner and Christ, the unsaved and the Saviour, judgement and mercy, the death of self and life in Christ. It may happen after a brief conversation, or after twenty or more years' prayer for an unconverted soul, but the ultimate surrender, whether witnessed by the evangelist here or not, is life's greatest gift both to the one who has sought and the one who is found. Heaven, so said our Lord, shares in the joy unspeakable, and it is the joy He offers to all His disciples here on earth that 'your joy may be full' (John 15.11).

'There is no fellowship with Christ that seems to me to be so vivid, so real to the soul, as when I try to win a soul for Him,' said Charles Haddon Spurgeon.

'There is no joy in all the world like the joy of bringing one soul to Christ,' says Professor William Barclay, University of Glasgow.

> *'Tis worth living for, this;*
> *To administer bliss*
> *And salvation in Jesus's Name.*

CHARLES WESLEY

It is true what all these three fine Christians say. Yes, it is gloriously true!

SOME EXAMPLES

*1. 'The Man Whom God Prepared for me'**

A short, tough-looking man – a boilersmith by trade, earning in those days (over sixty years ago) over £10 a week. He kept greyhounds and racing pigeons, gambled on horse-races and practically maintained a lad for flat racing on whom he gambled. Also, Geordie, as he was called, was one of the biggest drunkards on Tyneside.

It was my father, a Methodist Minister, who found Geordie tending his racing pigeons one Sunday, and asked him to come to the Men's Meeting. My father lovingly pursued his man for eight weeks and then, one night, Geordie – to use the phrase which stands for experience in which we must ever believe – *was gloriously saved*.

Some time after, Geordie heard that the young flat-racer was dying of consumption. He sought and found him, alone in a bare, cold, attic bedroom. After a few minutes' chat he left him, but returned with purchases which included coal and fruit, etc. When the fire was lit, Geordie sat down to talk.

As they talked, Geordie's mind became more and more uneasy. He felt that he ought to speak to the young man about his soul, but an unusual shyness prevented him. At last he rose to go.

'Ah, well, Aa'll away! Aa'll be back the morn!'

'S'long! Thanks for aal the things 'ee've fetched us! Mind you, it wes a grand thing fer you when 'ee ga convarted, Geordie!'

* John Wesley's description of Peter Bohler in his classic Journal, and a true description also of what Geordie was to me when I was a boy.

'By, it wes an' aal! The Lord's myed a mighty change i' maa life!'

'He has that. Aa wish He'd dee the syme fer me!'

'Wey, ax Him, man, an' He will. . . . Shall aa gan an' fetch sombody ti taak ti you, that knaas mair nor me?'

'Na, na, Geordie hinny; aa want nebody but ye.'

'Wey, ax Him yersel', then.'

'Aye, but aa divvent knaa hoo ti pray.'

'Wey, jist say the Lord's Prayer eftor me.'

Geordie knelt beside the sick man, and together they prayed the Lord's Prayer several times. It was the best that Geordie could do; but he yearned to bring this soul into the Light, and to do it single-handed. And God understood.

After several attempts the young man was able to repeat the prayer on his own: '. . . But deliver us from evil.' At the next visit a wonderful smile appeared on the disease-wasted face as the young man said: 'Geordie He's deen fer me what He did fer thee.'

Now, when the picture of Geordie comes to my mind, a man who became a dear personal friend of mine when I was not more than nine years of age, and remember that he could hardly read or write when he was converted, and that my father taught him the Lord's Prayer, how could I say – how could any Christian after seeing this true picture from life, say – 'It's not in my line?'

I couldn't say it to *His face*.

2. In a train, a few years ago

Early one Sunday morning I was travelling by train to a preaching appointment, and the only other occupant of the compartment was a man, a complete stranger. How we came to be on the same train and in the same compartment we both came to recognize as a wonderful example of His Divine guidance. Conversation led to the discovery that my acquaintance – now a beloved friend – was a widower, living alone some miles out of Newcastle, a non-churchgoer, and, like myself, old enough to draw the State (or 'Old Age') pension.

As we continued our talk together, I also discovered that he had once attended a 'Primitive Methodist Sunday school' and, in talking about his work in earlier years, that he had once had a foreman for whom he retained a great regard. I asked for the name of the foreman, who, he said, if he were alive must now be an old man. I said: 'He is, for I think the man you name is a member of my Tuesday evening fellowship in Newcastle, and he was eighty years old a few weeks ago.'

He promised to come and meet his one-time foreman and friend. The echo of a far-off Sunday school, a Christian foreman, the Methodist minister in the place where he lives, whom, in due course, I phoned giving him the name and address of my new friend and a message to deliver for me – all were used by the Holy Spirit in this link up in personal evangelism.

The result is that he began to attend church – after a lapse of *fifty* years – later, he committed his life to Christ in my home, and then not long after, was admitted into full membership of our Church at Corbridge-on-Tyne, and attended regularly the fellowship there. At a meeting of my fellowship in Newcastle he came one night when the subject of the conversation happened to be 'Spiritual Gratitude'. He was the last who desired to speak that night and he told the meeting how thankful he was to God that he had been 'brought home'. As he told of the way God had found and blessed him, all were greatly moved. A year later, he suddenly passed away – and to think that I might have been content to remain silent or pass a remark or two about the weather and leave it at that on a railway journey of less than one hour!

3. *In my study*

One of my friends, now a member of my Tuesday fellowship, came to me one Saturday evening, a complete stranger, feeling *desperately* needy, with this introduction: 'My doctor advised me to see you.' I made reply: 'Well, I'm no medical expert, but it must be because your doctor, whoever he is, knows that I know the Great Physician – tell me your need.' Drugs and medical treatment had not been without effect, but the doctor wisely recognized his inability to effect a real cure. The cure was not instantaneous, but the evidence of the Master's healing power is to be seen in a life now healthy and happy, and enjoying to this day the fellowship and service of Christ and His Church. That miracle of His grace and power took place more than twenty-five years ago.

4. *On a policeman's beat*

A businessman was in London over the weekend. He had no connection with the Church and Sunday was a long, weary day. Walking down Whitehall, he approached a policeman and asked if he would direct him to the nearest cinema. The policeman said he could direct him to a much better place. 'Continue down Whitehall,' said the policeman, 'bear right in Westminister Square, keeping the Abbey on your left, and round to the right you will see a large domed building – go in there and you will hear one of the world's greatest preachers. Goodnight, Sir.' The businessman accepted the invitation, entered Westminster Central Hall and shared in a service conducted by Dr Sangster. In that service God spoke to this man and he opened his heart to the Saviour.

5. In the rain*

On my way to preach one day in the town of Portsmouth, I stood in a doorway because of the heavy rain. Another man sheltered, too. I remarked on the weather, but as the conversation proceeded I told him of the errand I was on. He knew, it seemed, next to nothing about churches, but quite willingly accepted an invitation to come. He decided for Christ that night. It was all very simple and sweet.

But one thing he never seems to get over. 'Fancy standing up out of the rain,' he says, 'and all your life being changed because of that!'

6. In a service†

I remember a day I once spent in County Durham with a friend of mine – a coal-miner. He is a man in middle life now. Before his conversion, he was a drunken sot. He was a cheat as well. Playing once in a dominoes competition, he covered a dot with a bit of chewing gum and cleared the 'kitty' of £29.

He had a good mother and a good wife, and he came near to breaking the heart of both of them. One day his mother said to his wife: 'Leave him, Nellie. Leave him! He'll drag you to hell!'

But Nellie didn't leave him, nor ceased to pray, and

*From *Let me Commend*, by W. E. Sangster.
† From *Westminster Sermons* Vol. 1, p. 69, by W. E. Sangster.

one wonderful Sunday evening she had the answer to her prayers. Spent up and miserably sober, he yielded to her pleading and went with her to evening worship where a friend of mine was preaching his characteristically powerful evangelical word. When, at the end of the sermon, my friend made an appeal, Jack stumbled forward and asked God to forgive him.

What an hour! I think he only ever glanced back once . . . and it was but a glance! He was transformed in the astonished gaze of all the neighbourhood. In the passing of only a few years, the Holy Spirit wiped from his face all the marks of dissipation and made him radiant with an unearthly light.

When I first knew him, I had been ordained twice as long as he had been converted, and there are some things I can do, I suppose, that he can't do. But oh! there are many more important things that *he* can do which I can't do. It is wonderful to hear him talk to men who have missed their way; such love, such incisiveness, such skill with sinners. . . . I know he has travelled the road of Christian discipleship faster than I have done.

*7. In the home of the miner** (sequel to no. 6)

Facing me for my inspiration, as I sit at my desk in the office, is a photograph taken in the house of a miner in Durham, where a fellowship of some fifty members, many of them converted there, meet every Sunday night in order to gather strength for the coming week's witness. The photograph shows that almost all belong to just that class of young people with whom the Church is so greatly preoccupied. They have sent a missionary of their own to Africa, but they are all

* From *Bristol Fashion*, by Hugh Redwood.

missionaries where they live and work. They win their parents, their work-mates, the people they contact over the counter. Three of them are nurses in a hospital fifteen miles away, but they cycle that distance, when duty permits, to take their part in the fellowship meetings, and afterwards cycle back again. Thirty miles at the end of the day to meet with God in a miner's dwelling. Tell that to the empty down-town churches. Last year a team of these same young people spent several days in a Yorkshire town speaking for Christ in the market-place. Communists wanted to know who paid them, and learned that each of them put down £5 as his or her share of the expenses. Tell that to defaulting witnesses, and to those, if any, who still believe that religion, in a world like ours, is too sacred a thing to be aired in public.

8. On a bus

Some time ago, a man in my Fellowship Group gave thanks to God for the fact that, over the years, whenever I had been on his bus (he was a conductor), I had whispered to him, given the opportunity, 'I'm still praying for you', or, seeing him in the street, had always stopped to speak to him, concluding the conversation, however brief, with the same reminder. One December I said in one of these encounters: 'God will have His way with you, my friend, I am sure.' He laughed in disbelief, if not altogether in scorn, at the possibility of a life held fast for many years in the bondage of gambling and other sins ever being any different. Early the following year, God laid hold of him through the ministry of the Rev. Roland Brown (U.S.A.) and he was made anew.

I was told of his conversion on a Monday evening

(though no name was given, I felt it might be he)
and the next night, as I walked to my Fellowship
meeting, and prayed *en route*, I was led to make
humble claim to God that, if this man had been really
converted, he would make his way to our meeting that
night. Many of my personal prayers, and those of my
fellow members, become the corporate prayers of our
Fellowship Group, and for this man we had prayed
many times at that meeting. He was not there at the
opening hymn, nor after the prayer; hence, as I gave
out the second hymn, the devil whispered: 'How foolish
you were to make such a claim!' Then the door opened
a crack, and I saw part of his face, and, as we were
singing, I waved a welcome to him. Later, in our
Prayer Fellowship, he gave a glorious testimony of
thanksgiving to God.

At the end of the meeting he said to me: 'You didn't
seem surprised to see me.' 'No,' I said, 'I heard last
night that you had been converted, and I *knew* God
would bring you here tonight.'

9. *Through the out-reach of prayer**

My own brother prayed for me; he knew it was a
waste of time asking me to go to church or attend
evangelistic meetings, for I would not even discuss
Christianity. My brother and some of his friends made
a solemn covenant with God that they would pray every
day for my conversion. . . .

One evening I saw my brother going out with his
Bible under his arm, and, as he passed, I looked at him
with a very cynical expression on my face and said:
'Goodnight, brother; I hope you will have a time of

* Tom Rees of Hildenborough Hall gave his account of his
own conversion. Tom is a dear friend and relation of mine.

great blessing in your blessed meeting tonight.' He was a wise fellow he just took it from whence it came, gave me a smile and walked out. Less than twenty-four hours after that, without having spoken to a soul, I was down on my knees asking Jesus Christ to forgive my sins and, as I got up from my knees, a child of God, in the quiet of my room, God's Spirit told me to go straight to my brother's room and tell him I had become a Christian. . . . When I opened the door, he was sitting at his desk writing. I went in and said, 'Dick.' He did not look up, but went on writing. 'I've come to tell you,' I said, 'that I've become a Christian, I've given my life to Jesus Christ.' Very quietly, he took off his glasses, put his book down, and looked up to me and said, 'Oh, I'm not a bit surprised.' I got a shock. I said: 'You are not surprised! Why not?' He said: 'Well, you see, Tom, I have been praying for it.'

These are some examples of the fruit of personal evangelism.

TO GOD BE ALL THE GLORY.